Yoga for All

Yoga for All

Important note:
This book has been carefully compiled in line with current knowledge. However, no responsibility shall be taken for the accuracy of the information contained therein. The publisher and authors shall not be liable for any consequential damage resulting from the practical tips given in this book.
The advice contained in this book should not be followed in place of a medical examination. A doctor should be consulted prior to undertaking any self-treatment, particularly if you suffer from health problems, take regular medication or are pregnant.

TABLE OF CONTENTS

INTRODUCTION

Yoga, the life teaching originating in ancient India, is becoming increasingly popular. The number of yoga courses and workshops is on the rise, as is the provision of holidays geared towards yoga and well-being. But why are more and more people turning to yoga?

It is the desire for physical activity combined with relaxation of the mind, body and soul, as well as the longing to breathe freely again in these relentless times and to discover yourself. Acknowledging that many health problems are psychosomatic in nature, and knowing that a healthy mind is the foundation of our well-being, leads us to yoga. Yoga means a joining or unity of the mind, body and soul: a unity often disturbed by outside influences in our everyday lives. Yoga is among the most effective techniques for relieving mental and physical tension and therefore experiencing peace and tranquillity.

Relieving tension enables us to reduce our daily stresses and regain our balance. Yoga consists of a harmonious sequence of movements carried out with flowing breathing techniques, which have a positive effect on our physical awareness and our mood.

Yoga has nothing to do with acrobatics and its aim is not to achieve the most complex of postures. There are asanas (yoga poses) suitable for everyone: from children, teenagers and adults through to the elderly and the infirm. There are asanas for every ability.

This book tells you everything you need to know about yoga and its practice. It provides valuable advice on the effects of the asanas. You can use the exercises introduced in the Practice section, which include basic and follow-on exercises as well as a power yoga programme, to put together your own individual yoga training session.

Power yoga is a form of exercise based on the ancient Ashtanga yoga system, which is especially notable for its dynamic movements. The exercises are much faster and the priority, unlike many other forms of yoga stemming from Eastern religions, is not to withdraw inwardly from the world to prepare the mind for higher spiritual experiences, but rather to develop effective energy management. The programme is therefore particularly suited to those who are already very familiar with the basic and follow-on exercises, and want to reduce stress through physical exercise, while building up new energy levels.

HISTORY, PHILOSOPHY AND BENEFITS OF YOGA

The term "yoga" originates from Sanskrit, the sacred language of the Hindus and one of the formal languages still used in India today. Yoga, whose root word is derived from 'yug', 'yoke', means 'to join/unite', the union of mind, body and soul. Rishis, Indian sages and seers from the Indus valley, observed nature and, from their observations, they developed postures and exercises that allowed people to create a balance between the mind, body and soul, thus achieving personal unity. Yoga has been practised in India for more than 4000 years. It was the Sufis, free-thinking mystics, who brought yoga to many Far Eastern countries in around 1200 BC. Interest in yoga was aroused in the Western world at the beginning of the 19th century, when the first translations of old Indian texts by Western scholars were completed. At the end of the 19th century, yoga finally moved into the West. Initially, this was thanks to the numerous journeys, speeches and publications by leading yoga masters, then, later, due to the appeal of Asian cultures and the ease of travel to more distant countries.

Approximately 2500 years ago, Yoga first appeared in written form. Around the year 400 BC, the Indian scholar and philosopher Patanjali summarised this traditional philosophy system, which originated in India and is based on direct experience, in the form of aphorisms. Today, Patanjali's work, the Yoga-Sutra, is the most widely read classical yoga text. It comprises 195 aphorisms, referred to as sutras. Besides the philosophical and religious system of yoga illustrated here, it also includes statements in relation to the potential of the human mind, the causes of imbalance between the mind, body and soul, and how we can regain balance. Over time, from these aphorisms have developed various yoga paths, which coexist on an equal footing and pursue individual aspects of yoga. The best known are Hatha Yoga, Kundalini Yoga, Raja Yoga, Bhakti Yoga, Karma Yoga and Gyan Yoga.

Hatha Yoga is one of the most celebrated forms of yoga. It focuses on the body and includes predominantly static postures, Pranayama (controlled breath work), breathing exercises and relaxation techniques.

Kundalini Yoga is the yoga of awareness and channelling energy. Here the sequences mainly incorporate dynamically and energetically coordinated exercises that increase vital energy (prana), and have a cleansing, activating and, at the same time, relaxing effect.

Raja Yoga, also known as "the Royal Path", involves the development of willpower and energy, which is achieved by meditating on the chakras (energy centres in the body).

Bhakti Yoga is the yoga of devotion to God. The aim is to become one with creation and the Creator.

Karma Yoga, the yoga of selfless action and service, enables destiny to be seen as an opportunity. Karma Yoga can eliminate blockages that stem from selfish actions.

Gyan Yoga, the yoga of knowledge and wisdom, endeavours to discover the universal nature of time.

The art of yoga is, accordingly, the oldest traditional, holistic exercise system for relaxing, revitalising and energising the mind, body and soul. The essence of yoga is self-realisation, achieving a state of pure consciousness or enlightenment (Samadhi), the ultimate goal of yoga. For the yoga novice, this may seem like a remote prospect, but the initial aim is the path towards primary alleviation of the stress and tension that often puts a strain on our daily lives and throws us off balance.

First and foremost, yoga consists of three major components: the asanas (postures), Pranayama (conscious control of breathing) and, finally, deep relaxation.

The **asanas** ensure that muscles and joints are supple; they improve mobility of the spine, strengthen the internal organs, boost circulation and promote blood flow. These exercises relieve physical and mental tension and achieve inner peace and relaxation. When carrying out the asanas, it is important to pay full attention to and focus on each posture. This concentration allows the mind and body to connect, producing a meditation effect and demonstrating yoga's uniqueness.

Pranayama, the conscious control of breathing, is a fixed and important element of yoga, which is why each yoga session should begin with a breathing exercise. Only once we have perfected our breathing will all our body cells be supplied with sufficient oxygen and therefore cleansed. Conscious breathing helps us to overcome fear, anxiety and fatigue.

The perfect time for meditating
is in the early hours of the morning,
when our minds are still free and clear.

Deep relaxation concludes a yoga session and leads to the mind and body feeling calmer and more rested; stress hormone levels fall and inner blockages are dissolved. Deep relaxation has a balancing effect and focuses the mind. In yoga this is an active process, involving both the mind and body. Because tension and relaxation act as two opposing poles, the depth of relaxation is dependent on how intensively the asanas are performed. Deep relaxation can therefore only be achieved if the preceding tension is just as profound.

In principle, eight different aspects of yoga can be identified, which we will explain in more detail below. These are: behavioural rules, self-discipline, postures, breath control, sense control, concentration, meditation and enlightenment.

THE EIGHT LIMBS OF YOGA

The eight limbs of yoga are described in the well-known yoga sutras of Indian philosopher Patanjali and are the basis of the yoga system. According to yogic philosophy, these different limbs should be mastered in order to cleanse the mind and body, to become in tune with yourself and finally to achieve enlightenment.

The eight limbs of yoga include:
- Attitudes towards others (Yama)
- Attitudes towards oneself (Niyama)
- Body postures (Asana)
- Conscious breath control (Pranayama)
- Sense control (Pratyahara)
- Concentration (Dharana)
- Meditation (Dhyana)
- Enlightenment (Samadhi)

Yama – Attitudes towards others

Yama describes traits that should influence the way we interact with our surroundings and with others. Benevolence, compassion and respect towards others are associated with honesty in words, actions and thoughts. We should go through life as our true selves and in such a way that we are not obsessed with possessions, have no envy of others, do not steal nor have any kind of dependency. In our consumerist and materialistic society, this may seem difficult, but help is available from yoga itself, even if only for five minutes each day. Yoga, practised in the early morning, when our minds are still relaxed and free, supports us on this path. It is an inward path, that to our true selves. Gradually, we will start to notice that our values and thus our conduct changes towards ourselves and the world around us.

Niyama – Attitudes towards oneself

Self-discipline is an important constituent of yoga. It encompasses purity in relation to the mind and body, satisfaction, self-study, asceticism and devotion. We can experience inner purity and clarity of the mind by undertaking regular yoga exercise, being aware of our breathing and meditating. When doing so it is important that we do not worry too much and that we pay constant attention to our well-being. Initially, we may perhaps practise for just five minutes each day, but soon we will be exercising more frequently, intensively and regularly depending on our experience. Maybe we could get accustomed to taking a cold shower every morning, another yogic tradition. Not only does this freshen, energise and condition the body, but it also helps to prevent colds as well as heart and circulatory disorders. Self-reflection and meditation are a great help in finding contentment and in responding calmly to everyday life situations. Subjecting our thoughts and actions to criticism and studying philosophical writings support us in this, as does asceticism: an abstemious way of life suggests a conscious control of body and mind as well as meditation and a healthy, balanced diet. Those who have ever fasted know, from experience, how much clearer our perception seems after a few days. Devotion seems to be the most complex of all self-disciplines. In yoga this means devotion to God, following the inner voice and having confidence in the flow of life.

Asana – Posture

There are more than 200 different body postures. Using the asanas, we are able to train our physical flexibility, our muscles, organs and nerves. This allows us to achieve stability and harmonises body and mind. Conscious performance and correct breathing are important with all the asanas. These postures are predominantly carried out at a slow pace and are static, though there are also some exercise sequences that are flowing and dynamic. The effects of each of the asanas vary greatly. For each life situation there is a suitable yoga exercise, which both relaxes and strengthens us at the same time.

Pranayama – Conscious breath control

Breathing exercises are practised in yoga in which prana, vital energy, is consciously controlled and directed. In this context, yama can be translated as management or guidance. Breathing is controlled by the nervous system and is not subject to will. In conscious breath control, however, inhaling, exhaling and holding the breath are combined. This results in effective breathing, supplying all the body's cells with more oxygen and thus improving health. This conscious breath control enables a subtle sensation, uniting the mind and body, and providing a feeling of relaxation. This is also a perfect form of meditation for everyday life. So often we experience stress, fear and anxiety literally robbing us of our breathing. Longer, deeper breathing relaxes and centres us. There are various breathing techniques: long, deep breathing, full breathing, abdominal and diaphragmatic breathing, flank breathing and chest breathing. Full breathing is of particular importance. We take a closer look at this in the section on breathing. Take the time to learn these types of breathing as it will allow you to use full breathing in daily life situations where you need to practise long, calm breathing.

Pratyahara – Sense control

Pratyahara, the withdrawal and control of the senses, is a huge challenge for us in this modern, over-stimulated world. It involves guiding the senses from within and focusing on our own being. We must bear in mind, however, the stimuli that arise within us and distract us. Thus, Pratyahara means the internal and external stimuli to which our senses react in order to redirect or transform. Also, to perceive only what strengthens us and replace negative thinking with positive thought patterns. Focusing on our breathing and meditation are both beneficial here.

Dharana – Concentration

Concentrating the mind on one focal point is known as Dharana. To do this, it is important to be in a relaxed posture, focus your attention inwardly and have peaceful thoughts, which can be achieved through conscious and deep breathing. The focal point helps us to keep our thoughts on track. Various items can be used as possible focal points. We can concentrate our attention on an object or the flame of a candle, for instance. In yoga, Dharana is usually practised with the eyes closed, with the "third eye" – between the eyebrows – often being used as the focal point. Directing our attention to one of these points calms the flow of thoughts.

Dhyana – Meditation

Meditation is best described as immersion in the inner self. The aim here is to increase our consciousness and thus our awareness, to achieve a better understanding of ourselves. There are different meditation techniques, in which breathing and the sound of a mantra play a key role. Mantra can be translated as "projection of the mind". The well-known "Ave Maria" is a mantra, as is "Om", which means "everything that was, that is and that will be". Mantras are sung, thought or spoken during meditation and help to focus our attention. Once we have mastered the art of meditating and we have gained better self-awareness, Samadhi – enlightenment – follows.

Samadhi – Enlightenment

The ultimate aim of yoga is Samadhi, enlightenment. Samadhi is described as the deepest state of meditation, which leads to perfect unity with creation. It is the knowledge that everything is connected to everything else with no judgement or assessment. According to yogic tradition, God is the universe, is in everything and we are at one with God.

The imposing Manushi Buddhas from Elura in the Indian Federal State of Maharashtra represent the predecessors of Siddharta Gautama, the founder of Buddhism.

YOGA AND HEALTH

YOGA FOR HEALING AND MAINTAINING HEALTH

The body is our earthly temple, according to a yogic saying. As such, we must pay careful attention to our bodies. Yoga is a great benefit here. With the help of different postures and special exercise sequences, which are always combined with conscious breathing, we can preserve and regain mobility, strength and energy. Via this path, we can find our way towards relaxation, relieving our physical and mental tensions. There is hardly a more suitable form of exercise than yoga for reducing stress and offsetting the effects of our occasionally unhealthy lifestyles.

The body is a complex energy system, in which breathing, the heart beat and brain function are in constant and close interaction with each other. Through yoga, we introduce a harmonising process to this interaction, leaving no part of the body or the mind untouched. Mental blockages can also have negative impacts on our bodies. We often hear expressions such as: "That's getting me down", "That's breathing down my neck" or "That gets on my nerves". Yoga enables us to handle illness, fear, sadness or injury better by teaching us how to deal with the feelings that they provoke.

POSTURE

Correct posture is a fundamental aspect of the yoga poses. An upright and healthy body posture gives people a positive appearance: they appear taller and more relaxed. With an upright upper body, our breathing flows without restriction and the entire lung capacity is used. Various asanas performed standing up, such as the Tree, in particular affect the posture and sense of equilibrium that are essential for a balanced pose. In contrast, other asanas work on flexibility and an upright spine. Back pain caused by poor posture or sitting too long can be alleviated with yoga exercises such as the Cat.

MUSCLES

Our muscles are important energy bearers. This is why it is all the more important to train them because, without regular movement, muscles become weak and thin, and begin to lose their strength. Muscles generate an energy flow by constantly moving, which not only strengthens the muscles themselves but also the deeper-lying organs. To be able to understand this energy flow, it is essential to have some knowledge of the meridians. These are life force energy flows that run along certain pathways throughout the body. There are 14 primary meridians that are connected to each organ. If one of these meridians is blocked, the energy cannot flow along its predetermined pathway. This can result in an illness affecting the corresponding organ. Yoga helps us to strengthen our muscles and stimulate them. This promotes the flow of energy and thus supplies the organs.

Listen to your body's signals: strengthen weak muscles; stretch and relax shortened and/or tense muscles.

CIRCULATION, TISSUES, LYMPHATIC SYSTEM

Yoga is not only excellent training for your circulatory system: your muscles are moving when performing the yoga positions, which changes the position of the bones in relation to each other and increases pressure on the organs involved. This process is like having an internal organ massage. It enables deposits to be transported away from muscles and joints and allows them to move freely again. In addition, the metabolism is stimulated and digestive processes are activated. This internal organ massage is extremely important for the lymphatic and vascular systems. The function of both is to carry fluids away, depending on outside pressure and movement. For this reason, there are numerous exercise sequences for these systems. In order for the body's cleansing organs – skin, lungs, kidneys and bowel – to eliminate the freed waste products following the yoga exercises, you should relax after each yoga set and drink plenty of water to further support the excretory function of the kidneys.

NERVOUS SYSTEM

We are constantly being confronted with new challenges. Physical and mental over-exertion, too little time, pressure to succeed and over-stimulation are among the numerous stress triggers that can govern our lives. The outcome of these can be physical symptoms, ranging from heart and circulatory disorders to gastrointestinal complaints and migraines, and typical psychosomatic conditions. In addition to all this, mental illnesses such as depression or anxiety are common in the modern age.

Yoga can also be beneficial because it is a holistic exercise system encouraging relaxation and revitalisation for the mind, body and soul. Stress caused by tension can be minimised or even eliminated by practising meditation and deep de-stressing.

If you have a psychiatric illness (or epilepsy) and/or you are taking psychopharmaceuticals, yoga should be practised only after consultation with a doctor and with the guidance of a yoga teacher.

Experience relaxation and a zest for life.

YOGA FOR BEAUTY

Ancient yogic writings describe the ideal image of a beautiful body: not too fat and not too thin, powerful but not too muscular, a slim waistline and supple limbs. The skin should be glowing with a fresh complexion and the eyes should be bright and clear. Not only is there a wide range of poses to help achieve this goal, but cleansing exercises for the stomach and bowel have also been created, based on current knowledge, which bring relief to the body. In addition, there are a number of asanas that stimulate digestion and the metabolism, enabling the inner body to regain or maintain momentum. Again, there are further exercises to strengthen the back and promote the development of stronger muscles, which not only give the body support but also produce a healthy, upright posture. This results in the body attaining the right balance and paves the way to individual physical harmony.

YOGA FOR EVERYDAY ACHES AND PAINS

Everyday aches and pains can be actively counteracted by different yoga exercises. Headaches can be relieved or avoided by stretching and regularly training the spine. This releases pressure from the spine, improves blood circulation and regulates blood pressure. Regular relaxation by consciously controlled breathing combined with meditation is also important. Through practising continuous breathing exercises, not only will the sinuses be free, breathing will become deeper and more rhythmic. Hyperventilation and asthma improve or do not even occur. The heart also benefits from regular exercises and effective breathing. Blood circulation is stimulated and blood pressure falls.

The improvement in posture achieved by practising yoga has a positive impact on hip joints, knees and ankles, which remain flexible and supple or regain these properties. The tendency for back pain may also diminish due to greater spinal flexibility, which can be achieved through regular extending and stretching.

Digestion is improved since effective breathing stimulates the digestive system and the stretching and strengthening of the abdominal muscles has a massaging effect on the internal organs. A positive side effect here is that the abdominal muscles remain strong and flat.

Despite all the positive benefits of yoga, it should be borne in mind that certain yoga poses should not be practised, or should be practised very carefully, by those with certain health conditions. Therefore, before you start your yoga training, you should consult your doctor.

YOGA AND NUTRITION

THE CORRECT DIET ACCORDING TO THE RULES OF YOGA

As we have already mentioned, having the right attitude towards yourself – Niyama – is one of the eight limbs of yoga. As well as being one of the rules of yoga, this also means that you should follow an appropriately moderate lifestyle, especially in terms of a good and healthy diet.

The ancient Indian rules for yogis prescribe a very specific diet with special foods to keep them young and fit. Of course, not all of these rules can be transferred to Western lifestyles, as some of these foods may not be available. One rule, however, is the same for Western and Indian yogis – only with a healthy diet can those practising yoga achieve the desired results for the mind and body, namely yoga and diet – physical and mental equilibrium.

HEALTHY NUTRITION

The following recommendations for a healthy diet can easily be applied – both by people who practise yoga as well as those who generally want a healthy diet.

1. Through our diets, we consume vital nutrients, which the body needs to maintain vitality and immunity and to remain mentally fit. Unnatural foodstuffs mostly contain additional substances such as taste enhancers, preservatives, etc., which burden the body. Certain actions destroy vitamins and minerals, so the body does not receive sufficient nutrients. As a result of this, you may feel tired, exhausted or lack concentration and often you eat more than you actually need. This leads to obesity.

2. Avoid eating too quickly. Chew slowly and carefully: each bite should be chewed into small pieces in the mouth and mixed with saliva. "True" yogis place their cutlery to the side after each bite, close their eyes and focus on chewing.
When you have enough time to eat, you also avoid these mistakes:

3. Eating too much. The feeling of fullness starts only after around 20 minutes. Eating quickly means that a lot of food can be consumed in 20 minutes. For the most part this ends in a feeling of fullness and digestive problems, because food is often not chewed properly in the mouth and all the digestion has to take place in the stomach and bowel.

4. Only eat when you actually feel hungry. People's biorhythms are different. Not everybody needs to eat a warm meal at twelve noon and a meal at seven in the evening. On the other hand, some people skip breakfast. Nutritional and physiological principles do

not recommend this as the body needs the foundation in the morning to be able to have enough energy for the day. Coffee, tea or yoghurt and/or fruit juice will, however, offer some nutrients. It is best to listen to your body and its needs. When you're hungry, eat.

WHAT SHOULD YOU EAT?

- A good and healthy diet consists of plenty of fresh fruit and vegetables. Processed foods should be restricted. Experts recommend five portions of fruit and/or vegetables a day. This could be a portion of fruit muesli in the morning, for instance.
- White flour products have no nutritional value. These should be substituted with wholegrain products: wholemeal bread, wholemeal pastries, wholemeal pasta and brown rice.
- We do not need white sugar in our diets since standard, refined sugar is completely void of nutrients. The body does not need it; it generates sugars from grains. If you need to use sugar, switch to unrefined.
- Mass-produced fizzy drinks contain artificial flavours, lots of sugar and few nutrients. These should be replaced by mineral water or diluted fruit juices.
- Not all fats are the same. It is important to pay particular attention to non-hydrogenated fats and unsaturated fatty acids. Animal fats are rich in unhealthy saturated fatty acids, which cause an increase in cholesterol levels and blood pressure. These place stress on the body rather than relieve it. Vegetable fats, particularly cold-pressed oils, contain high levels of unsaturated fatty acids, which is where the nutrients are. Only certain types of fish, for instance salmon, contain valuable omega-3 fatty acids.

MEAT – YES OR NO?

This issue has divided opinions for some time. For those practising yoga: you can generally eat meat if it is right for you. There are no rules for this. Many people respect the animal and thank it for having given its life for human consumption.

Eating meat has both its advantages and disadvantages. Meat contains essential nutrients, such as protein, which the human body needs. Of course, this can be replaced by vegetable proteins. Too much animal protein places a strain on the human metabolism, which may trigger illnesses. When we eat meat, we consume all the substances that the animal has been given, including any medication or toxic ingredients in its food.

For meat-eaters, we recommend:

- eating meat only once or twice a week and just in small amounts.
- that meat should be fresh and if possible well-cooked or roasted. Raw meat contains more harmful bacteria than cooked meat.
- eat meat only if you know from where it originated. This means not eating meat from large-scale livestock farms but from organic farms with controlled, organically grown feed.

FASTING AS A CLEANSER

Doctors and dietitians recommend fasting once or twice a year. For those practising yoga it is pretty much essential, for most yogis it is a given. Fasting supports the effect of the asanas in an impressive manner.

Fasting has nothing to do with hunger, which discourages many people from undertaking a fast. The absorption of nutrients is deliberately controlled through a specific intake of fluids. This means a basic cleansing of the mind and body.

All healthy people can fast. A consultation with your doctor is recommended beforehand.

TIP: When fasting it is important to drink plenty, to avoid any strenuous exercise and get plenty of sleep.

YOGA PRACTICE

KEY FEATURES OF THE ASANAS

According to traditional yoga teaching, we must first be in control of our bodies before we can achieve a higher level of spiritual awareness. We can train this control using the asanas, which make our bodies flexible and supple, and optimise vital energy. Out of around 80 basic positions, approximately 30 are carried out regularly. The different postures include standing and sitting positions as well as those on your knees and lying down.

STANDING EXERCISES

Not only do the standing asanas require strength and stamina, but they also promote these qualities. The upright position, also known as the Tree, teaches us to stand with awareness, trains our sense of balance and encourages good posture. Standing positions that are practised regularly strengthen the leg and pelvic muscles as well as the spine. They tighten tissue, promote circulation in the legs and gradually reduce unpleasant fatty deposits in the buttocks. Health problems such as back or shoulder pain, neck tension, as well as a rounded or hollow back, can be reduced.

EXERCISES SITTING DOWN OR ON YOUR KNEES

Exercises in the sitting position or on your knees have a variety of effects. Depending on the assumed position, muscle groups can be extended and stretched, which releases tension in the back, neck and shoulders. This leads to greater flexibility in the spine and pain in this area can be reduced or eliminated altogether. Extending the back muscles and the groin provides us with greater mobility in the hip joints. Rotating movements stimulate the internal organs, which boosts the metabolism and promotes circulation. Rotating positions that expand the chest area have an effect on the lungs and improve breathing. Other asanas support blood flow in the head and encourage deep relaxation as well as increased powers of concentration.

EXERCISES IN THE LYING POSITION

Performing asanas when lying down is an excellent relaxation exercise. Simply lying on your stomach relieves tension in the entire body and not only helps with back pain but also deepens breathing in the chest. It provides new energy by relaxing the mind.

Lying on your back is also very effective for relieving tension and facilitates both partial and full breathing. The lying down exercises in their different versions strengthen the entire spinal column, loosen the vertebrae in the lower back and, performed carefully, help with vertebral complaints. Rotating exercises stimulate blood flow and the metabolism as well as supporting breathing. Extending and stretching the upper body is beneficial if you have breathing complaints and relaxes the neck and the upper back.

SAVASANA – DEEP RELAXATION

Each yoga sequence should end with some deep relaxation. Savasana is known as the Corpse pose and produces total relaxation of the mind, body and soul. It is also an excellent exercise if you suffer from insomnia.

Lie on your back and cover yourself up so that you do not get cold; otherwise the muscles are not able to relax. Tuck the chin in lightly, stretch the back of the neck, relax the arms at the side of the body with the palms of the hands facing upwards. Place your legs parallel to each other with the heels touching, allow your feet to fall loosely to the side. Pay attention to the symmetry of the body and align your body in a straight line from head to toe.

Close your eyes and observe your breathing. Consciously inhale and exhale and allow your thoughts to drift through your body, starting with your feet, through the calf, thigh and up to the pelvis, until finally reaching the head. While doing so, pay attention to the individual muscles, gradually releasing the tension in them by consciously exhaling. Notice how the entire body relaxes, so meditate while concentrating on your now free-flowing breathing. To end the exercise, inhale and exhale deeply several times. Stretch your body comfortably from head to toe and raise yourself up using your side.

PERFORMING THE ASANAS

Asanas consist of static postures, dynamic movement sequences and relaxation exercises. The common feature of these exercises lies in the fact that they are always built on three basic principles: conscious posture, breath control and concentration on the exercise.

- Before you adopt a pose, familiarise yourself with each individual step of the exercise. Only once you have done this should you assume the position. When performing complex exercises, it is helpful to visualise the posture or exercise sequence beforehand. Close your eyes and carry out the impending exercise in your head.
- Then carry out the actual exercise and remain in it. In this phase, it is important to concentrate on the exercise and the flow of your breath as well as the correct breathing control. Some asanas have a specific breathing rhythm, which should be followed as far as possible. If there is no particular mention of a rhythm, breathe consciously, in a relaxed manner and at your own pace.
- To increase concentration on the exercise, it helps to close your eyes. Make sure, however, that you are comfortable doing this, as it can be better to keep your eyes open when it comes to rotary movements or standing postures.
- For the most part, the duration of the asanas is predetermined. Try to stick to this time as far as possible but always listen to your body when performing the exercise. Stretching pain or some other kind may develop in the muscles and tendons in untrained bodies. Listen to these signals and slowly come out of the respective exercise, with no sudden or rapid movements, and relax. The key factors in determining how long you exercise for are your physical constitution and your desire!
- At the end of the exercise remain in the position for a few more minutes, feel the effect of this exercise on your body and relax briefly.

Opening the chest during a yoga exercise allows the breath to flow freely.

Allow yourself to be aware of this individual experience and listen to your mind and body when performing the asanas. Not every exercise is right at any given time. Your current physical and mental state is always an important factor. Be mindful of the balance of the asanas as each posture has a specific effect on your body and soul.

THE YOGA SESSION

Each sequence of yoga exercises is a journey to discover ourselves. Embrace this and begin your journey with a ritual: sit in your favourite place, listen to some quiet meditation music, light a candle, an aroma lamp or an incense stick and leave your daily cares behind you.

- Each yoga position is introduced with a short relaxation exercise in the sitting or lying position combined with conscious and deep inhalation and exhalation. As you relax, close your eyes and settle into your own private yoga lesson.

- The next step is the warm-up stage. This promotes circulation and loosens muscles, joints and the spine. Whether extending, stretching, dancing, walking or hopping, do not forget to be aware of your breathing. You should not exercise without warming up or stretching beforehand; otherwise, you are at risk of injury.

- The physical exercises should be enjoyable, carried out in their predetermined form and with ease, in accordance with the detailed description at the beginning of the section. When performing the individual exercises, pay attention to their smooth, harmonious rhythm.

- Relaxation exercises, such as the deep relaxation described, round off the end of a yoga lesson.

Important: Do not eat a large meal less than two hours prior to your yoga lesson as the digestion process blocks energy and different exercises put pressure on the digestive organs. Drink plenty of still water during your yoga session to support the excretion of toxins released when performing the exercises.

BASIC YOGA GUIDELINES

The following section contains tips and suggestions to help you enjoy your yoga sessions in complete harmony. This section tells you when, where and how to exercise, how often you should train and when it is best to abstain from exercising.

WHERE AND HOW?

Ideally, you will have your own room for exercising. If not, find an area of around four square metres in your apartment or house where you will not be disturbed. In good weather, you could of course use your balcony or garden. It is important that the area is quiet and warm – and, above all, draught free.

You can purchase special non-slip yoga mats as well as large, soft blankets and fleeces, which are ideal for exercising. Always make sure you have a solid floor to exercise on so that you do not slip when performing your standing exercises. If you are exercising while sitting on the floor, you should sit on a cushion or on a folded blanket since the knees should always be lower than the hips in the sitting postures. When you are exercising, we recommend that you wear loose, comfortable clothing that you feel good in. It is better to exercise in bare feet – do not wear shoes or stockings.

WHEN?

Early in the morning, during the so-called "ambrosial hours", is the optimum time to start your yoga programme. Initially this may take a lot of effort, but you will soon learn to appreciate the health benefits that come from early-morning exercise. You will then be ready to tackle the new day head on with renewed strength, restored balance and filled with energy.

Early evening is also an ideal time for exercising, particularly when you come home exhausted and tense after a stressful day at work. Depending on which exercises you decide to do, you will feel either re-energised afterwards and ready for more exercises, or relaxed and ready for undisturbed sleep. Yoga is also recommended when you yearn for relaxation or want to activate your vital energy.

HOW OFTEN?

Practise yoga at least twice a week, at most four times, for 30 minutes at a time. This allows your muscles to recover and better adapt to new exercises. If it is not always possible to stick to your exercise routine, do not become disheartened: simply continue your routine the following day. Even if you have to start again, you must stick with it!

WHEN TO ABSTAIN?

Yoga is a great healer but there are situations where it must be practised slowly and carefully:

- viral infections, febrile illnesses etc. or when taking antibiotics
- extreme exhaustion
- heavy menstrual bleeding as exercising can increase the blood flow
- after a long break from exercising

If you have any of the following health problems, you should completely refrain from yoga in the first instance and only start exercising again after consulting your doctor:

- persistent and/or severe backache (vertebral disc damage, sciatica, lumbago etc.)
- severe neck pain (whiplash etc.)
- inflammation in the body
- high blood pressure and hyperthyroidism
- following surgery
- in the last trimester of pregnancy

If you experience any sudden pain during your yoga session, stop the exercise immediately by slowly coming out of the posture. Contact your doctor for an opinion.

If you are suffering from a psychiatric illness, yoga should be practised only after consultation with your doctor.

BREATHING

We have also discussed how important breathing correctly is for our well-being. But what is correct breathing? It means full inhalation and exhalation, using the entire lung capacity so that all the body's cells are supplied with sufficient oxygen. For this reason, the chest (chest breathing), ribs (flank breathing) and the stomach (abdominal or diaphragmatic breathing) should all be involved. Ideally, we should take in up to 2.5 litres of air in one breath. In our daily lives, we make do with around half a litre, as our activities are predominantly carried out sitting down and we move around too little. This results in lack of concentration and fatigue. Yoga teaches us to focus on our breathing, improving and deepening it. Deep and strong breathing energises and relaxes the mind, body and soul.

FULL BREATHING

Full breathing is a combination of abdominal, flank and chest breathing. Before carrying out full breathing, you should practise each of these breathing techniques separately and only then should you combine them. With each of these techniques, always breathe in and out through the nose. The breath is filtered and warmed in the nose and an important energy exchange takes place in the membranes of the nasal walls, which are well supplied with blood. Practise these techniques with your eyes closed so that you can focus better on your breathing. You can find an accurate description of both abdominal and flank breathing on pages 32 and 34.

CHEST BREATHING

Chest breathing can be practised in either the lying or upright position. Place both hands on the upper part of the chest so that these also touch the collar-bone. Exhale and then, as you inhale, feel the flow of breath in the upper part of the lungs and chest. The chest and collar-bone rise as you inhale; make sure that your shoulders do not rise at the same time. As you exhale, the chest and collar-bone are lowered again. Start with six breathing cycles and slowly increase these to ten.

PRACTISING FULL BREATHING

Once you have managed the individual breathing techniques, you can combine these to practise full breathing. This takes some practice, but the full breathing technique will become easier.

Lie on your back, close your eyes and focus on the flow of your breathing. Breathe out fully and allow your breath to flow initially into the lower part of the lungs and then into the entire lung area: curve your stomach outwards, stretch the ribs, expand the upper chest area and raise your collar-bone. Slowly exhale again, gradually relaxing the respiratory muscles while doing so. Lower the chest and collar-bone, then the rib cage and finally the stomach. It is essential when carrying out full breathing that you maintain the correct sequence. As you inhale, stretch or expand the stomach, then the ribs and finally the chest. As you exhale, first lower the chest, followed by the rib cage and finally pull the stomach in. Start with six full breathing cycles and gradually increase the number. At the end of the exercise, you should relax for a few more minutes, inhaling and exhaling consciously and slowly.

Breathing will become more even, deeper and longer the more you practise.

EXHALING

As previously mentioned, most people do not fully inhale and exhale. A typical insufficient breathing technique would be, for instance, when the out-breath is shorter than the in-breath. This means that too little carbon dioxide is being exhaled and the carbon dioxide left in the blood will gradually block the body's channels. This is why it is important to be conscious of our breaths in and out.

Place your hands on your chest or stomach and be aware of your breathing.

Breathing exercises: Abdominal breathing

- Stand upright with your spine straight. Only then will you be able to breathe freely.
- Inhale slowly and deeply, allowing your stomach to curve outwards as you do so. Then allow the air to flow into your chest.
- Exhale slowly and evenly. To support your breath out, tighten your stomach muscles lightly together; the stomach sinks again and the chest relaxes.
- Breaths in and breaths out should be the same in length.

Meaning:

In our everyday lives, our breathing is often very superficial, especially when we are flustered or tense. A few deep breaths, carried out consciously with abdominal breathing, work wonders here. Abdominal breathing is also a component of full breathing, which is a combination of chest, abdominal and flank breathing.

Effect:

Deep breathing improves oxygen supply: it relaxes and soothes.

Repetitions:

You should take at least ten deep breaths. Stick with it, provided you feel well.

Limitations:

This breathing exercise is so easy that you can integrate it into your routine several times a day, preferably more often rather than less often.

Breathing exercises: Alternate nostril breathing

Nadi Shodhana

- Close the right nostril with your right-hand thumb and exhale slowly and deeply.
- Inhale deeply through the free left nostril and then close the left nostril using the ring finger on the right hand. Hold your breath and count to eight.
- Remove your thumb from the right nostril and exhale completely.
- Now inhale deeply through the right nostril, then close the right nostril with your thumb, hold your breath as described and remove the ring finger from the left nostril to exhale. Now inhale again on the left and repeat the cycle.

1

2

Meaning:

The Sanskrit description of this exercise signifies that the Nadis are cleansed and harmonised by alternate nostril breathing. Nadis are the energy channels passing through the entire body, along which vital energy (prana) flows.

Effect:

The aim of alternate nostril breathing is to accumulate vital energy and calm the mind.

Repetitions:

It is essential that you leave plenty of time for the breathing exercises. Start with six repetitions of the four phases. Increase the intensity over time by breathing more deeply, though no more than ten times. Inhalation and exhalation should be around the same length on both sides.

Limitations:

If you feel dizzy when doing the alternate nostril breathing, return to normal breathing. If you have a stuffy nose or nasal congestion, you should refrain from doing this exercise.

Breathing exercises: Flank breathing

- Stand in the straddle position with the ends of the toes pointing outwards. Support yourself by resting your left hand on the middle of your left thigh. Point your right arm outwards.
- Now inhale slowly and deeply through your nose and exhale at the same slow pace. As you exhale, lean your upper body slowly to the left-hand side.
- Inhale again and slowly return to the starting position (straddle position), right arm pointing out to the right.
- Then switch to the other side (left arm pointing out to the left, right hand on the right thigh) and repeat the breathing process on this side.

Meaning:

The different "ventilation" in the two lungs has an ancient tradition. The preliminary breathing exercises end with this one and allow you to address the asanas with belief and knowledge. Flank breathing is part of full breathing, though in the latter the position as presented in the image is not adopted but rather the flow of breathing is simply channelled through the flanks so that the chest expands.

Effect:

Correct breathing means breathing fully and deeply. Many people have forgotten this. Flank breathing cleanses and detoxifies our organs and at the same time has a relaxing effect on our bodies.

Repetitions:

Carry out the flank breathing exercises three times on each side.

Limitations:

Anybody can carry out the flank breathing exercise. In rare cases, you may feel dizzy if you are unaccustomed to intensive breathing. Should this occur, return to your normal breathing pattern.

WARM-UP

Do not forget to boost your circulation before starting the exercises: walk, jog or hop on the spot. You could also dance if you prefer. Remember to do the stretches and extensions.

Turning the Head: Right and Left

- You can decide whether you prefer to do this exercise standing up or in a comfortable seat. Whichever variant you decide on, it is important that your posture is straight and upright.
- Inhale and, as you exhale, slowly turn your head to the right as far as it will go.
- Again, inhale slowly through the nose and turn your head back to the front.
- Then repeat the same sequence on the other side. Inhale and, as you exhale, turn to the left and then back to the front as you inhale.

Effect:

Much stress is often placed on the cervical spine and its muscles in daily life; these react by tensing up. Our first exercise aims to counteract this. At the same time it prepares you for later (balancing) exercises (asanas).

Repetitions:

You should leave plenty of time for doing the prepared exercises. Turn your head to each side three times.

Raising and Lowering the Head

- Inhale deeply through the nose and gently lean your head back into your neck so that it is comfortable.
- Exhale again. As you do, tuck in your chin towards your breastbone. This is carried out in one smooth motion; the speed is determined by your breathing.
- During mobilisation, the three repetitions mentioned are sufficient for those who are more advanced. In later asanas, however, the intensity must be increased.

Meaning:

This gentle warm-up exercise aims to stimulate the mind and body and, at the same time, release tension. It specifically mobilises the cervical spine. This exercise is an excellent initial interplay between conscious breathing and movement.

Repetitions:

Repeat the sequence three times. Leave plenty of time for the exercise. It is precisely this connection with breathing that prevents the exercise being carried out too quickly.

Limitations:

If you have severe problems with the cervical spine area, you should be particularly careful when leaning your head backwards. Do not gaze all the way up to the ceiling: just raise your head gently and slowly.

Rolling the Shoulders

- In an upright position or standing up, slowly pull both shoulders upwards (towards your ears) and inhale deeply through the nose.
- Then pull the shoulder-blades back and press them down again so that you are making one large backwards circle. Exhale deeply through your nose as you do so.

Meaning:

Even if you have no complaints about your shoulder-joints, you should be aware that it is these joints that most often suffer wear and tear. They have a very large socket and movements are conducted by ligaments and muscles. The backward shoulder rotations straighten up your posture – and an upright posture goes hand in hand with self-awareness and self-confidence.

Effect:

The entire shoulder-blade and chest areas are loosened up by the gentle rotations, preparing you for later (core-strengthening) asanas.

Repetitions:

Beginners can repeat these exercise sequences three to five times.

Limitations:

If the exercise is controlled and carried out more slowly, there are no risks whatsoever. You can by all means practise the shoulder rotations more often throughout the day, even when sitting at your desk.

BASIC STANDING EXERCISES

The Mountain *Tadasana*

- Stand upright. Your feet should be parallel to each other and a hip-width apart.
- Hold your entire spine in its natural posture. Consciously straighten yourself up, hold your head upright and feel the lengthening in your spine.
- Then pull the shoulder-blades back and downwards, thereby widening the chest.
- At the same time, raise your arms and stretch them out to the sides, at an angle of 45° rather than a right angle, so that your fingertips are at the side of you, pointing towards the ground. Inhale deeply as you do so and hold the position for the space of a few breaths.

Meaning:

The Mountain appears to be an easy position at first glance. You must, however, stand like a mountain, upright and without moving. You will soon discover that this position is very demanding and requires concentration.

Effect:

This standing position exercise aims to calm the mind and body. It opens the chest area, facilitates breathing and supports an upright posture.

Repetitions:

Repeat switching from tension and relaxation four to six times. Over a period you can increase the number of repetitions as well as the intensity of the muscle contractions.

Limitations:

The Mountain can be practised by anyone, without limitation. Ensure that the shoulder-blades are only pulled back as far as the natural position of your spine allows. If you pull them too far back, you will over-arch your spine. You should avoid doing that at all costs.

The Tree *Vrikshasana*

- Start with the easy version of the Tree (Fig. 1). Only once you feel confident should you attempt the advanced version (Fig. 2).
- Standing upright, transfer your weight to the left leg and place the right foot down onto the calf of the left leg (Fig. 1).
- Allow the knee of the supporting leg to bend slightly to provide a secure footing.
- Then place the palms of your hands together in front of your chest. Hold this position for 3–4 breaths and lower your arms as you exhale.
- Then repeat the Tree on the other side (right supporting leg).

Meaning:

The Tree position is reminiscent of a tree rooted to the ground – through the feet – and growing high up into the sky (arms). This position conveys a wonderful feeling of inner peace and tranquillity.

Effect:

This exercise has a stimulating effect on the brain brought about by the balance organ in the inner ear. In the same way that your hearing capacity deteriorates with age so does your sense of balance. This is also connected to a lack of exercise in our daily lives. Apart from children playing, who still balances on a tree? The Tree not only trains our senses of balance and concentration but also has an overall calming effect.

TIP: If you do not feel very confident to begin with or keep losing your balance, gently place the tips of your toes on the floor next to the other foot.

The Warrior *Virabhadrasana*

For beginners (Fig. 1):

- Stand in an upright position with your legs wide apart. Keep your legs straight.
- As you inhale, raise your arms above your head, keeping the palms of your hands facing upwards until they come into contact with each other.
- Turn the left foot inwards and the right foot outwards. Turn your right leg and torso to the right, away from your hip. Then bend the right leg and push your hips downwards.
- Remain there for a few breaths and then stretch the right leg as you inhale. Turn yourself back to the front, lower your arms and calmly exhale as you do so.
- Now do the exercise on the other side of your body.

For more advanced students (Fig. 2):

- Performing the movement is different in that it builds up more of the muscles in the buttocks before leaning the arms and upper body back a little more.
- Look up at your hands.

Repetitions:

Hold the Warrior pose for at least ten calm breaths. You can carefully increase the stress over time by making the lunge deeper.

TIP: Imagine pulling yourself up to the ceiling with your fingertips, while at the same time pulling downwards into your hips.

The Warrior II *Virabhadrasana*

- Stand upright with legs wide (legs wider than your shoulders).
- Stretch your arms out to the side at shoulder height and turn the palms of your hands downwards.
- Then turn your right foot outwards. Exhale and transfer your body weight to the right leg by bending it. Feel the stretch through the left inner thigh.
- Hold the position for 20–30 seconds and then stretch your right leg until you are back in the starting position.
- Repeat the exercise on the other side.

Meaning:

Virabhadrasana was a great warrior in an epic poem written by the Indian dramatist Kalidasa in the 5th century. The position constitutes a strong, stable pose, which involves various postures.

Effect:

The exercise strengthens the leg muscles and helps create greater stability.

Repetitions:

When performing the Warrior, more important than the number of repetitions (three to five is sufficient) is ensuring your footing is secure and self-confident.

Limitations:

Keep your shoulders low, i. e. avoid lifting your shoulders up as this leads to tension. Simply imagine that your fingertips are being pulled from opposite sides and your torso will straighten up beautifully. Make sure, especially if you have knee problems, that when the leg is bent the knee is positioned over the heel. If the knee pushes too far forward, this will increase stress on the joint!

The Triangle *Trikonasana*

For beginners (Fig. 1):

- Stand in an upright position with legs straddled wide apart. Bend your right leg.
- Bend your upper body to the right as you exhale, with your outstretched left arm pointing upwards and your right forearm resting on the middle of your right thigh.
- Remain in this position for a short time and slowly return to the starting position as you inhale.
- Then repeat the exercise on the other side of your body.

For more advanced students (Fig. 2):

- Stand in an upright position with legs straddled wide apart. Stretch your arms out.
- As you exhale, lower your upper body down to the right side as far as you can go and allow your right hand to slide down your leg towards the floor.
- Use your ankle to provide balance and focus on maintaining an outstretched, straight posture.
- Remain in this position for a short time and slowly return to the starting position as you inhale.
- Then repeat the exercise on the other side of your body.

Effect:

The Triangle strengthens the leg muscles. The flank muscles on your torso are extended, stimulating diaphragmatic breathing.

Repetitions:

Three alternate repetitions are preferable.

Limitations:

The beginners' version can be easily carried out by anyone. The extended Triangle should be practised only by more advanced students, who already have excellent body awareness and no back problems!

BASIC FLOOR EXERCISES

The Cat *Marjariasana*

- Get onto all fours (hands directly beneath the shoulders and knees directly beneath the hips).
- Look downwards and keep your head in line with the spine. Inhale deeply and lightly arch your back (Fig. 1).
- As you exhale, raise your entire spine upwards and allow your head to hang down loosely (Fig. 2).
- Bring the speed of the movement into line with the pace of your breathing.

Meaning:

It is obvious how the name for this exercise came about: the smooth movement sequence is similar to that of a cat and the typical arch it creates with its back when enjoying a stretch.

Effect:

The cat pose makes the entire spine from the neck to the lumbar region more flexible, improves the circulation of the back extensors (i.e. the left and right muscles of the backbone) and loosens the muscles between the shoulder-blades.

Repetitions:

Do three sets of repetitions, from the starting position in the "cat arch" and back again.

Limitations:

The Cat is an exercise for everyone, provided that there are no severe vertebral disc problems. It is important that you approach the stretch carefully and do not make any sudden movements. The back should be curved evenly, i.e. in a well-formed semi-circle. This is easier said than done since individual areas of the spine (e.g. the neck) are able to bend much more easily than others. It is useful if you can look at yourself in the mirror to check as you are doing this.

The Dog *Shvanasana*

For beginners (Fig. 1):

- The starting position for the Dog is on all fours, i.e. supported by the hands and knees, with the hands beneath the shoulders and the knees beneath the hips.
- Lift your knees from the floor and push your buttocks up towards the ceiling. Now try to lower the heels carefully towards the floor.
- Then attempt to push the chest back towards the thighs. Remain here for a moment and then lower the knees back down to the floor.

For more advanced students (Fig. 2):

- Your starting position is the Four-Limb Staff, i.e. the hands are beneath the shoulders, legs outstretched and the feet positioned.
- From this position, push your buttocks up towards the ceiling. Then press your heels towards the floor. Keep your legs outstretched. Push your chest downwards towards the thighs. A fundamental difference from the beginners' exercise is the fully outstretched legs.

Meaning:

In this exercise, you are imitating a stretching dog. If you can imagine this, the movement will come more easily to you.

Effect:

The Dog stretches the muscles of the cervical spine and the shoulder muscles. The exercise helps with general fatigue because it slows down the heart beat, and invigorates the brain and nervous system.

TIP: The position appears very complex at the start of the exercise. Initially, leave your legs bent for as long as it feels comfortable. You should, however, be able to feel a distinct pulling sensation. Over time, you will be able to stretch the leg more, press your heels further into the floor and push the upper body further towards the thighs.

The Half Lord of the Fishes *Ardha Matsyendrasana*

For beginners (Fig. 1):

- Sit on the floor and stretch out your legs.
- Then cross your left foot over your right leg. Point the knee upwards.
- Place your left hand behind your body. Stretch your back as you do so.
- Your right arm is stretched across your left leg. As you exhale, twist backwards so that you can see over your left shoulder.
- Remain in position for a few breaths and go back to the original position in the return sequence, in preparation for working the other side (right foot over left leg).

TIP: Ensure that the spine is upright and straight. Press both buttocks into the floor. Turn your torso only as far as feels comfortable.

For more advanced students (Fig. 2):

- When performing the exercise, more advanced students can also bend the right leg. Make sure, however, that both buttocks remain on the floor.

Meaning:

This asana has taken its name from the legendary founder of Hatha Yoga, Matsyendrasana. The Half Lord of the Fishes is one of the most traditional twisting exercises, with a positive impact on the internal organs.

Effect:

The Half Lord of the Fishes invigorates your flank breathing and stimulates the upper abdominal organs. This has a positive impact on your digestion. At the same time the muscles are strengthened, the torso is straightened and the deep-seated buttock muscles are stretched.

Limitations:

You should not practise the Half Lord of the Fishes if you have back problems or sciatica.

The Tortoise *Kurmasana*

- Sit upright and bend your legs. Place the soles of your feet together.
- Grip your ankles from underneath and slowly lower the cervical spine and head as you exhale.
- Remain in this position for a few breaths and then, as you inhale, slowly roll your spine back down vertebra by vertebra.

Meaning:

This exercise emulates a tortoise, hiding its head from the world outside and withdrawing into its shell. It directs its attention inwards towards itself.

Effect:

The Tortoise stretches the muscles in the area of the lumbar spine, loosens muscles in the cervical spine area and improves circulation in the internal organs. All the leg muscles, especially those in the inner thigh (adductors), are stretched intensively. The cervical spine is straightened and the chest is open, which intensifies breathing.

Repetitions:

In a calm and smooth movement, switch between the upright and forward-bending position three to four times.

Limitations:

Not suitable if you are pregnant or if you have severe back problems. Beginners can make sitting easier by spreading the knees. They can start on a chair and then later move to a cushion.

FOLLOW-ON STANDING EXERCISES

If you would like to focus in particular on the follow-on exercises during your training, start as usual with the warm-up and then select three asanas from the basic exercises. You will then be well prepared for your follow-on training.

The Sun Salutation for Beginners *Surya Namaskar*

The Sun Salutation is the classic pose among yoga exercises and an ideal warm-up for the asanas (postures). There are a total of twelve postures that flow easily into one another and form a harmonious movement sequence. In Hindu mythology, the Sun God personifies good health and long life. In the Sun Salutation, the rising sun is greeted. It therefore fits best into the exercise programme in the early morning.

- Place the palms of your hands together in front of the chest. Exhale deeply as you do so.
- Bring your arms above your head in a large outwards arch and inhale as you do so.
- Exhale as you lower your hands down to your thighs, bend your legs (push your buttocks backwards/downwards in the process).

- Place your hands in front of or next to your feet on the floor.
- Take a large step backwards with your right foot. In doing so, raise the chest and head a little and inhale deeply and calmly.
- Now place the left foot behind you, next to the right foot, and exhale as you do so. The entire body should now be stretched out in a straight line. Inhale deeply.
- From the outstretched position, push your buttocks upwards and exhale as you do.
- Bring the left foot back to the front underneath the upper body.

TIP: Make sure that in this phase of the Sun Salutation your back is straight when doing this posture.

10

- Take the right foot towards the left so that the feet are next to each other.
- From this supported squatting position, place your hands on your thighs one after the other.
- Straighten the upper body slowly in one smooth movement and, at the same time, stretch your arms above your head in a large arch. Inhale deeply as you do so.
- On your next exhalation, place your hands together and draw your clasped hand in towards your chest.

Effect:

As a complete movement sequence, the Sun Salutation:

- Stimulates breathing, circulation and digestion; therefore has a general reviving effect
- Mobilises all the major joints (especially the spine, hip and shoulder-joints). All the important muscle groups are involved.
- Improves concentration by combining breathing and movement

Repetitions:

Beginners should repeat the Sun Salutation sequence two to three times.

Limitations:

This beginner's version of the sun salutation is also suitable for individuals with back or knee problems.

TIP: Initially, exercise very slowly. The faster you perform the Sun Salutation over time, the greater stress you will feel.

The Balancing Stick *Utthita Satyeshikasana*

- Transfer your weight onto the left leg and gently stretch out your other leg behind you, still supporting yourself on the tips of your toes.
- Now transfer the entire weight of your upper body, stretching both arms slowly forwards.
- Try to bring yourself into a balanced position, i. e. bend your upper body and raise the leg stretched out behind you in such a way that the arms, torso and free leg form a horizontal, straight line. Then practise the balance on the right leg.

Meaning:

The Balancing Stick improves our sense of balance, which is often given little consideration in daily life and deteriorates with age (in the same way as our hearing does). The explanation for this is not only the fact that circulation within the hearing and balance organs deteriorates with age but also that in daily life we have very little interest in our balance.

Effect:

The Balancing Stick invigorates the muscles in the legs and buttocks, strengthens all the muscles on the back of the body, trains the sense of balance and has a relaxing and harmonising effect once you become accustomed to adopting a calm stance.

Repetitions:

Repeat the exercise on each leg two to four times, for as long as you feel comfortable.

TIP: At the beginning of the exercise, it is sufficient to lower the upper body only to a point at which you feel comfortable. The torso and the free leg should always form a straight line. After some practice, you will definitely be able to form a horizontal line. If you have any initial problems with the Balancing Stick, you can use a chair to help you.

The Eagle *Garudasana*

For beginners (Fig. 1):

- Start by standing straight with your feet a hip-width apart. Transfer your body weight to the right leg, raise your left foot and place it across the right thigh.
- Cross your arms at chest height and intertwine your fingers. Hold this position for a few breaths and then switch to the other leg.

For more advanced students (Fig. 2):

- The standing position as well as the arrangement of the arms and hands remain the same (see Fig. above). Now further increase the intensity by bending your supporting leg considerably more and then winding the crossed leg around the supporting leg.

Meaning:

This exercise is named after the mythical eagle Garuda, who has the body of a human but the head and wings of an eagle. The exercise requires good stability, balance and powers of concentration.

Effect:

The Eagle improves blood flow in the legs, strengthens the thigh muscles, boosts circulation and loosens the muscles between the shoulder-blades.

Repetitions:

Come out of the Eagle pose if you feel your supporting leg tensing up. This exercise is less about the number of repetitions and more about carrying out the posture correctly and with intensity. Over time, you can gradually increase the bend in the supporting leg.

TIP: When you actually bend the supporting leg, you can gain a very secure footing. As with all the exercises that require a sense of balance, it may be helpful to focus your eyes on a specific point.

The Low Lunge *Anjaneyasana*

For beginners (Fig. 1):

- Kneel down on the floor and bring your right foot forwards on the floor. The right knee should remain behind the right toes. Take your left leg back.
- Take your arms above your head and place the palms of your hands together. Look straight ahead.
- Clearly feel the stretching effect in the hip area. Push your hips forwards and this feeling will intensify. Remain in this slightly pushed forward position for three to four breaths.

Meaning:

For Indians, the Low Lunge embodies the feminine side of the person. The position for the Low Lunge opens the chest and thus has an effect on your heart's energy.

Effect:

The Low Lunge demands a sense of balance but even more so a general flexibility, especially in the hip flexor muscles in the back leg. The cervical spine is aligned at the same time.

Repetitions:

Practise the position as described, with the left foot forwards.

Limitations:

If you suffer from knee problems, the knee on the front bent leg should always remain behind the toes.

For more advanced students (Fig. 2):

- Start the Low Lunge in the same way as the beginners' version. However, take your rear leg much further back.
- Bring both arms above your head and place the palms of your hands together.
- Tense your buttocks and lean back slightly. You should clearly feel the stretch in the hip flexor muscles.
- Look upwards and follow your hands. Intensify the stretch by tensing the buttocks tightly.
- Remain at maximum stretch for three breaths and then return to a more comfortable position.

2

TIP: The more advanced you are, the further you can lower the hips, making it easier to look up towards your hands.

The Half Moon – Variation *Ardha Chandrasana*

- Kneel down and straighten your upper body.
- Now stretch out your right leg to the side and take both arms above your head so that the palms of the hands are touching.
- Then lean your upper body to the right-hand side and briefly hold the position. Bring your upper body back to the middle, lower the arms and draw your right knee back to the centre.
- Repeat the exercise on the other side.

Meaning:

This asana is based on the real half moon. It affects the lateral trunk muscles as well as different abdominal organs.

Effect:

The Half Moon strengthens the hip muscles of the bent leg, while at the same time stretching the hip muscles of the outstretched leg.

Repetitions:

Repeat this two to three times on both sides of the body.

Limitations:

The Half Moon can be carried out by anybody, without restriction. If you experience pain in the knee joint of the bent leg, place a cushion underneath.

FOLLOW-ON FLOOR EXERCISES

The Tiger *Vyaghrasana*

- Get down on all fours (see the Cat).
- Exhale as you pull your left knee towards your head and make yourself rounded.
- Then, as you inhale, stretch your spine and your left leg. Your head should fall back in line with the spine. Hold the position and your breath for a moment and then return to the rounded position as you breathe out.
- Repeat this exercise in one calm, smooth movement and switch to the other leg.

Meaning:

This is a dynamic and powerful variation on the previously described Cat pose. The exercise has taken its name from the tiger indigenous to India, a particularly noble and athletic large cat.

Effect:

The Tiger strengthens the buttocks and thigh muscles and increases flexibility in the spine. This exercise is therefore perfect for offsetting the effects of sitting in the office all day!

Repetitions:

Switch between the rounded back and the stretched position three times. Increase the exercise to ten times per side.

Limitations:

The Tiger is suitable for everyone, apart from those suffering from severe back problems. Important: it is better to carry out this exercise too slowly rather than too quickly. It should be a slow, controlled movement: do not make any dynamic movements. Allow the pace to be set by your own breathing.

The Four-Limb Staff *Chaturanga Dandasana*

For beginners (Fig. 1):

- Support yourself on your forearms and knees. Slowly stretch the knees so that your legs are away from the floor.
- Tighten your abdominal muscles (draw in your navel) and press the shoulders away from the ears.
- Your entire body should now be in a line: shoulders – buttocks – feet.
- Hold this position for around ten seconds, then slowly bend the legs, placing the knees down again. Relax briefly.

For more advanced students (Fig. 2):

- Support yourself on your hands and knees. Slowly stretch the knees so that the legs are away from the floor.
- Tighten your abdominal muscles (draw in your navel) and press the shoulders away from the ears. The entire body should form a line, i. e. the buttocks should be directly between the shoulders and the feet. Bend the arms slightly.
- Hold this position for ten seconds, then slowly bend the legs, placing the knees down again. Relax briefly.

Meaning:

This support exercise ("floor posture") stabilises the front of the torso, i. e. the chest, stomach and hip flexor muscles.

Repetitions:

Switch between resting and tensing three to four times. Increase the tension phase over time, so that you are in the Four-Limb Staff position for longer.

Limitations:

True beginners should stay in the holding phase for the space of two to three breaths and only increase this phase over time. There are no real limitations, however, and you should consider incorporating this exercise into your individual yoga programme every time.

The Locust *Schalabhasana*

- Lie down on your front on your mat. Extend your arms along your body with your palms facing upwards. Use your chin to support your head.
- Gently raise your pelvis and slide your hands in the space between your thigh and your groin. If you wish, you can form your hands into fists. You can, however, also keep them flat, with the palms facing upwards.

- Now breathe in, tense your body and lift your legs. As you do so, push yourself with your hands or fists as far as possible off the floor.
- Hold this position for at least five seconds without breathing. The chin remains supported on the floor.
- Breathing out, slowly allow your legs to lower. Remove your hands from under your thighs and lie them comfortably next to the body.
- Turn your head to one side and relax.

Meaning:

The Locust is one of the classical yoga poses. Its execution requires a degree of strength, experience and discipline.

Effect:

The exercise strengthens the muscles in the lumbar spine and pelvis and has a preventative effect for individuals prone to slipped discs. The buttocks, abdomen and upper thighs are strengthened.
The blood supply to the head is stimulated, while the pelvic organs, digestive organs and bladder, as well as gland activity, are also stimulated. The blood supply to the legs is increased, helping to prevent varicose veins.

Repetitions:

To begin with, it is advisable to repeat the exercise daily. It will then soon be possible to achieve the Full Locust.

Limitations:

The same limitations apply as to all exercises that are designed to strengthen the spine.

The Upward Plank *Purvottanasana*

- Sit on the floor with your legs stretched out in front of you and support yourself with your hands behind your buttocks.
- Now slowly lift your buttocks and push your hips towards the ceiling – far enough for your body to be in a straight line.
- Focus your gaze upwards.
- Hold your position for a few breaths and then return to the floor.

Meaning:

The Sanskrit name of this pose means "stick position". The entire body is supposed to be as rigid as a stick or plank.

Effect:

The Upward Plank, like all postural exercises, is primarily intended to strengthen. It tones the arms, shoulders and muscles around the shoulder-blades. The thoracic spine is aligned – an important step towards good posture.

Repetitions:

Alternate slowly three times between the lower position and the stretched-out position.

Limitations:

Because the Upward Plank places a lot of strain on the wrists, if you have any wrist problems, such as tenosynovitis, you should not do this exercise or you should shorten it considerably.

TIP: You can make this exercise easier the first few times you do it by supporting yourself not on your hands, but rather on your elbows.

The Stretched-Out Peacock *Uttana Mayurasana*

- Lie on your back on your mat. Stretch your legs out in front of you. Stretch your arms out to the side.
- As you breathe in, bring your legs together from the toes to the thighs.
- Now, with both legs still stretched out, lift them a few centimetres off the ground and briefly maintain this position.
- Now bend your legs and place your feet on the floor.
- Raise your heels and pull your feet up towards your buttocks as far as you can. Then set down your feet.
- Now lift your buttocks, your lower back and thoracic spine as far as you can off the ground.
- Lift your heels off the ground again. Also lift your arms and support your lower back with your hands. Try to push your thoracic spine further off the floor as you do so.
- Lower your heels.
- Maintain this position for at least 20 seconds.

- To come out of this pose, carry out the movements in reverse order, starting by lifting your heels and slowly lowering your thoracic spine, lumbar spine and then buttocks.
- Relax. Feel within your body whether this exercise has had any effect.

Meaning:

The Stretched-Out Peacock is a good counter-movement to the candle pose or headstand. Some people will be familiar with it from their school days. It requires a degree of body control.

Effect:

The exercise strengthens the spinal column and maintains its mobility. It has a strengthening and harmonising effect on the central nervous system. It also strengthens the gluteal muscles and tones the tissue. In addition, the wrists are strengthened.

Repetitions:

The exercise should be carried out slowly. Maintain the static phase for a few breaths.

Limitations:

People with back problems should consult their doctor before carrying out this exercise.

The Wind-Relieving Pose *Pavanamuktasana*

- Lie on your back, stretched out, on your mat. Flatten your neck area towards the floor.
- Align the arms along the body with the palms facing downwards and then, as you breathe in, bring the legs together from the toes to the thighs.
- Raise your extended right leg a few centimetres off the ground and briefly hold this position.
- Bend your right leg and place your toes on the floor.
- Move your toes towards your buttocks as far as you can.
- Lift your toes off the floor and move your leg towards your head.

- Breathing out, stretch your arms out towards the ceiling up to the height of your bent leg. Turn your palms so that they face each other, clasp your knee and pull it towards your chest while breathing in.
- Breathing out, lift your head and move your forehead towards your knee.
- Hold this position for at least ten seconds. With each breath out, try to move your forehead a little more towards your knee.

- Come out of the pose by carrying out the same movements in the reverse order and relax.
- Carry out the exercise with the left leg.
- As a variation, hold the un-bent leg a little off the floor during the exercise. This also allows you to sit up from your supine position.

Meaning:

This exercise is known as a wind-relieving pose since it is ideal as an immediate remedy, for instance for digestive problems. It is also a good counter-posture to the Cobra and the Locust.

Repetitions:

Repeat the exercise with the right and left leg alternately. Repeat it up to three times in succession, as you wish.

Effect:

This exercise has a strong effect on the pelvic organs. It helps with digestive problems such as bloating and the increased build-up of digestive gases. It also improves the activity of the digestive system and bladder function as a whole. It helps relieve back pain, fortifies the lumbar spine, strengthens the neck and abdominal muscles and relieves tension in the neck and shoulder area.

The Fish *Matsyasana*

- With your legs stretched out, lie on your back and place your hands with the palms facing downwards under your buttocks.
- Shift your weight onto your elbows, raise your head slightly and lift your rib cage to form a hollow under your back.
- Carefully lower your head and shift your weight onto your buttocks.
- Continue to breathe calmly and come out of the position carefully.

Meaning:

The Fish is an effective exercise for relieving the everyday tension that builds up, particularly in the muscles of the shoulders and neck.

Effect:

The pose relieves and relaxes the entire cervical spine and helps with muscle tension in the neck area. The widening of the rib cage makes breathing easier, which has a beneficial effect on individuals with asthma and respiratory problems. The Fish also increases the flow of blood to the head, stimulates the thyroid gland and regulates the metabolism.

Repetitions:

Allow plenty of time for this exercise and start with four to five repetitions. If you feel able to do so with time, you can increase this to up to twelve repetitions.

Limitations:

If you have any health-related cervical spine restrictions, you should first consult your doctor.

Variation:

Experienced individuals can move their heads all the way backwards and then lie their skull carefully on the floor.

The Plough *Halasana*

- Lie on your back on your mat. Your legs are extended and held together. Rest your hands alongside your body, with your palms facing downwards.
- Now, breathing out, lift both legs, breathe in and out twice and tense your abdominal and leg muscles.
- Support yourself with your hands on the floor, lift your buttocks and lower back, and breathe out.
- Lower your legs behind your head towards the floor. Keep your legs stretched out and bend your hips.
- Touch the floor with the tips of your toes and place the backs of your feet on the floor. Your back should now be completely off the ground. Your weight should be resting on your shoulders and the back of your head.
- Stretch out your arms and hands forwards away from the shoulders. Hold this position for at least ten seconds.
- To come out of the position, lift your legs off the floor and unroll your spine vertebra by vertebra. Lower your legs slowly towards the floor. It is important to do this slowly; the spine must not jar on the floor and your head should not lift up off the ground.
- Relax and feel the benefits of this exercise in the resting pose.

The Plough – Variations *Halasana*

- For experienced individuals: carry out the first six steps as described on page 71.
- Bend the knee behind your head towards the floor, spread your legs and try to place them on the ground next to your ears.

- Carry out the first six steps as described on page 71.
- Support your back with your hands so that it is completely straight.
- Push both legs, stretched out, as far as you can to the right. Keep your toes on the floor. Maintain this position for at least ten seconds. Then push your legs to the left while breathing out.

- Carry out the first six steps as described on page 71.
- Now spread your legs as far as you can, keeping your toes on the floor.
- With a circular movement, move your arms backwards until you can touch the tips of your toes with your fingers. Grasp your toes.

Meaning:

Halasana, the Plough, is the only pose that the yogis named after a tool. It belongs to the forwards-bending poses and is often carried out in conjunction with the shoulder stand.

Effect:

This pose firms and strengthens the muscles of the neck, shoulder and abdomen. It lengthens and strengthens the spine, relieves tension and ensures good elasticity; it tones the thighs and hips.

It ensures a good supply of blood to the head, thereby alleviating headaches.

The internal organs are stimulated and new energy flows through the body.

The nerves are strengthened.

The endocrine glands and the thyroid gland are stimulated, while the breakdown of fat cells is accelerated. The pose therefore indirectly regulates weight.

Repetitions:

To begin with, this pose is unfamiliar and, for many, unpleasant. This will change if you perform it daily. Advanced students relax in this pose after the shoulder stand.

Limitations:

People with back problems or slipped discs should avoid this exercise. The position is also not advised for people with thyroid disease or acute illness. The Plough can increase bleeding during menstruation.

TIP: If you find the pressure of the mat or floor too uncomfortable, you can place a blanket under your neck and shoulders.

The Reclined Bound-Angle Pose

Supta baddha konasana

For beginners (Fig. 1):

- Lie relaxed on your back, bend your legs and tilt your knees outwards.
- Place your hands on the insides of your thighs and now breathe deeply in and out using your diaphragm. Close your eyes.

For more advanced students (Fig. 2):

- Start the Reclined Bound-Angle Pose on your back, like the beginners. Then also grip your ankles and roll them together.
- Lift your head off the floor and hold this position for a few breaths.
- Then unfold back in a calm and flowing movement until you are once again in the beginners' position.
- Alternate a few times between the exercise for beginners and that for advanced students.

Effect:

This exercise provides energy and vitality. Specifically, it widens the pelvis and loosens the muscles in the lumbar spine area. It also stretches the majority of the adductor muscles (muscles on the inside of the upper thigh).

Repetitions:

Beginners can remain in the supine position for ten to fifteen breaths. Advanced students can repeat the alternation between the two positions eight to ten times.

Limitations:

Take particular care if you have back problems.

The Crocodile *Nakrasana*

- Lie on your back and stretch your arms out to the side. The palms of the hands should face upwards.

- Extend your right leg and place your left foot on the floor. Now slowly push your left knee to the right (over the right leg) and turn your head to the left as you do so. You will find this exercise to be like a twisting of the entire backbone.

- Breathe in deeply, hold your breath for a moment and then, as you breathe out, turn your head in a gentle movement to the right and your leg/knee correspondingly to the left. With this twisting movement, your pelvis will move too, i. e. only one of your buttocks will remain in contact with the floor.

- Repeat the exercise on the other side.

Meaning:

The Crocodile is an exercise that has a particularly intense effect on the spine. It prevents back problems, but is also useful for treating them. It is found to be beneficial by both beginners and more experienced students.

Effect:

The Crocodile stretches and relaxes the muscles of the cervical spine. It makes the lower back mobile and stimulates the activity of the kidneys.

Repetitions:

Repeat the change from one side to the other at least six times.

Limitations:

Although the Crocodile is very useful for preventing back problems, people who already have back pain should carry out this exercise with care. People with slipped discs should avoid this exercise.

The Foetus *Garbhasana*

For beginners (Fig. 1):

- Sit comfortably on your buttocks and hug your bent legs.
- Place your forehead on your knee and allow yourself to gently rock backwards until you feel the relaxation between your shoulder-blades.
- Breathe in and out deeply and hold this position for at least ten breaths.

For more advanced students (Fig. 2):

- Assume the knee position. Slowly put your weight on your heels and carefully incline your upper body forwards.
- Now place your forehead on the floor in front of you and move both of your arms backwards, placing them alongside your body. The palms of the hands should face upwards.
- Hold this position for a few deep breaths.
- Then set yourself back upright. Imagine you are "unfurling" like a rolled-up fern leaf.

Meaning:

This asana, which is easy to understand even for newcomers to yoga, is also known as the "child pose". This position allows you to retreat into yourself and switch off. The version for beginners is very different from the exercise for more advanced students.

Effect:

Both positions of the Foetus pose have a relaxing effect on the entire body. The muscles between the shoulder-blades and the neck muscles are also stretched. The Foetus is a renowned asana for relieving stress.

Repetitions:

Remain in this position for at least ten calm breaths. Do not be hurried by any type of clock. If, however, you feel pain in your comparatively markedly bent knees, you should stop the exercise.

Limitations:

With the Foetus pose, it is important to use a soft mat. People with knee problems should not perform this exercise or, if they do so, should put their weight very carefully on their heels.

The Lotus (comfortable) *Muktasana*

- Sit on the floor. Straighten your back and allow your shoulders to relax and lower.
- Bend one leg and then the other. As you do so, move your heels as close to your body as possible.
- Bring your middle finger and thumb together (mudra) and focus on relaxation and deep, calm breathing in and out.

Meaning:

The upright seated position has been an important element of meditation in yoga throughout the ages. Today, there are still many people for whom sitting on the floor is normal and sitting on furniture is the absolute exception. Habituation from a young age enables even older people to sit in such a way with ease and not find it uncomfortable. The Lotus position symbolises rootedness and stability in our foundations.

Effect:

The Lotus position, even in its simple version, calms the mind, promotes an erect posture, slows down the metabolism and corrects the position of the pelvis.

Repetitions:

With time, it should be possible to maintain the seated position for at least a quarter of an hour.

Limitations:

The knee joints in particular are bent a lot in the Lotus position. For this reason, people with knee problems or bad varicose veins should approach this position with considerable care and stop the exercise immediately if they feel pain.

Prone Position *Makarasana*

- Lie on your front. You will find it easier to relax if you place a rolled-up hand towel (or neck support) under your ankles. Some also feel better in this position with a rolled-up hand towel under their groin.
- Bring your arms together over your forehead until your hands overlap. Place your head in your hands and turn it slowly to the side. Remain in this position for a few breaths and then turn your head to the other side.

Meaning:

This relaxation exercise has an effect on the entire body. It is the ideal follow-on exercise in that it re-opens the body and deepens your inner calm. It is particularly suited to people who prefer to sleep on their stomachs.

Effect:

By lying on your stomach, you are calming your mind and recharging yourself with new energy.

Repetitions:

Remain lying on your stomach only for as long as you feel comfortable doing so. Even beginners should have no difficulties with ten repetitions.

Limitations:

Lying on your stomach is suitable for everyone, without limitations. All that matters (and this affects all movements of the cervical spine) is that you do not turn in sudden, jerky movements.

The Corpse *Savasana*

- Lie on your back in the most comfortable position for you and close your eyes. Straighten your body.
- Breathe consciously and place both hands on your abdomen – this helps you to consciously feel your breathing. Stretch your legs out, touch your heels together and allow your feet to fall loosely to the side.

- Meditate on the flow of your breathing and allow your thoughts to wander through your body. Start with your feet, travel up through your legs to your pelvis, then on to your upper body and finally to your head. Release any tension in your muscles with conscious breaths in and out.
- At the end of the relaxation phase, extend your arms over your head, stretch out like a cat waking up and consciously make yourself alert and active again.

Meaning:

Savasana literally means "corpse-like posture". You do not, however, have to imagine yourself entering an endless sleep. Relaxation is much more effective if you close your eyes and imagine that you are resting in a wonderful place somewhere.

Effect:

Savasana should truly relax you and restore the energy you have lost in your body, mind and soul through day-to-day stress.

Repetitions:

Relax in the Corpse position for as long as you feel comfortable doing so. For most people, ten minutes are enough.

Limitations:

The Corpse pose is one of the few positions that can truly be assumed by everyone without any limitations.

10-MINUTE PROGRAMME

As already mentioned, it is a good idea to practise yoga for half an hour at least twice and at most four times a week. Sometimes, however, our lives are such that we do not have enough time to devote ourselves to training with this level of intensity or frequency, and sometimes we need a physical and mental break from the stress of our everyday existence. You can put together your own exercise programme from the basic and follow-on exercises to suit your needs and the time you have available. To help you, we have assembled a few different short programmes, each lasting around 10 minutes, comprising a variety of focal exercises that you can use as a basis for ad hoc quick yoga breaks. No matter how pushed for time you are: never forgo the warm-up before starting your exercises. It is better to miss out one of the suggested poses if you are short of time. Equally, you should avoid exercises that you find unpleasant or even painful. After your training session, rest for a few minutes in the relaxed Corpse pose (see page 80).

BACK PROGRAMME

Lack of mobility is the number one cause of back problems, which are now among the most common conditions affecting the developed world. Especially if your work restricts you to "sitting still", you will come to appreciate the beneficial effects of the following exercise sequence.

- Warm-up (see pages 35–38)
- Balancing Stick (page 56)
- Cat (page 46)
- Tiger (page 62)
- Four-Limb Staff (page 63)
- Locust (page 64)
- Upward Plank (page 65)
- Stretched-Out Peacock (page 66)
- Foetus (page 76)

SHORT PROGRAMME FOR STRENGTHENING THE CORE

These exercises are intended to improve posture and body tension, and strengthen the abdominal muscles. They also reinforce your spine and make you fit for the stresses of everyday life.

- Warm-up (pages 35–38)
- Balancing Stick (page 56)
- Wind-Relieving Pose (page 68)
- Upward Plank (page 65)
- Four-Limb Staff (page 63)

SHORT PROGRAMME FOR IMPROVING MOBILITY

People who sit for long periods are more likely to "seize up". The following exercises will promote suppleness in your everyday movements and help you to tackle problems and difficulties in a more relaxed manner. They also prepare you well for (re-)starting sporting activities.

- Warm-up (pages 35–38)
- Sun Salutation (page 52)
- Dog (page 47)
- Low Lunge (page 58)
- Half Lord of the Fishes (page 48)

SHORT PROGRAMME FOR BALANCE TRAINING

The following asanas will help you specifically improve your sense of balance, co-ordination and confidence of movement, which becomes increasingly important, especially as we age. These exercises will help you bring your body and mind back into equilibrium.

- Warm-up (pages 35–38)
- Warrior (page 42)
- Tree (page 41)
- Eagle (page 57)
- Balancing Stick (page 56)

SHORT PROGRAMME FOR RELAXATION

These exercises are ideal for situations where you feel overwhelmed, stressed and exhausted. Treat yourself to a little time out so that you can tackle the rest of the day refreshed and in a positive frame of mind.

- Warm-up (pages 35–38)
- Cat (page 46)
- Foetus (page 76)
- Crocodile (page 75)
- Lotus (page 78)

POWER YOGA

DYNAMIC STRESS REDUCTION

Once you are sufficiently familiar with the asanas in the basic and follow-on exercises and are able to practise the poses successfully, you can introduce a little variety into your yoga training with the power yoga programme below. The programme is comprised exclusively of asanas with which you are already familiar and, thanks to its dynamic sequence of movements, helps considerably towards the regeneration of your energy reserves through "active relaxation".

Power yoga developed at the start of the 1990s in America and its aim is to promote physical as well as mental strength. Its roots lie in the millennia-old Indian Ashtanga tradition, and in its current form it addresses Western needs for relaxation, physical balance and revitalisation.

The meditations to deepen relaxation that are so key to yoga are performed at the end of the exercises and thus have a positive effect on the nervous system.

The way of connecting individual positions into a flowing whole, so characteristic of power yoga, offers something special – the exercises demonstrate in the truest sense of the word how energy can be collected and controlled. The exercises function like a dance, in which the body moves in a balanced and at the same time very powerful way. Breathing and movement are perfectly harmonised. Although the speed of the exercise sequence is quite fast, the individual remains very calm and focused.

The flowing sequences of movements in power yoga are synchronised with breathing. The individual changes their posture in harmony with a specific breathing pattern, thereby releasing energy. A few asanas are held for several breaths while tensing certain parts of the muscles (static muscle contractions). By synchronising breathing and movement, energy is dynamically increased and the body is not over-burdened or unequally stressed. The individual aspects of this breathing technique (ocean breathing), as well as the particular features of the exercises themselves, are set out below, along with techniques that can be used to direct and control the flow of energy in the body through specific key points in the body (bandhas).

FREE-FLOWING ENERGY, STRENGTH AND CONCENTRATION

Positive inner "energy management" is becoming more and more important for individuals.

To be able to process the stimuli that swirl around us and interact constructively with other people and our environment, we need methods that promote alertness and presence.

Power yoga is ideal for this, as it removes energy blocks and energises the body and mind. Years of practice are not necessary. The effects can be felt after just the first few exercise sequences: pent-up energy is released and individuals begin to feel "whole" again.

The connection between the flow of movement and controlled breathing techniques generate heat during power yoga that circulates through the body throughout the exercise, detoxifying it and cleansing the mind. You will become aware of your physical capacities, i. e building strength, which in turn has a positive effect on your psychological well-being.

The flow of energy and the development of heat cannot be achieved in power yoga without concentration: which in this case means attentiveness, self-awareness and a focus on what is happening within your body. In power yoga, this is accomplished through conscious breathing.

The more practised you are at the exercise sequences, at contrasting the muscles in the poses you maintain and tensing the "bandhas" (about which more will be explained later), in order to maintain heat, the more evenly you will be able to concentrate on your breathing and your body.

Power yoga becomes effective when breathing, movement and static muscle tension work together in perfect harmony. You should not expect this result to occur straightaway, however. That said, if you are able to co-ordinate the individual elements of the exercise sequences, you will enjoy the full beneficial effect of power yoga. To do this, you will need to train and practise concentrating.

OCEAN BREATH AND THE BANDHAS

For humans, the importance of breathing goes far beyond our purely biological needs. Not only is it essential for health, but it also connects us with the outside world, with other people and with each individual cell in our bodies. Conscious breathing heightens our awareness of our own bodies. It stimulates the senses and key physical functions.

If we are aware of our own breathing, our level of consciousness increases. Deep breathing clears the mind, calms the nerves and provides the body with energy. It has a positive effect on the body's energy centres, or chakras. If these energy zones are addressed directly, we connect with our inner core, we sense ourselves and we are able to better identify our creative abilities. We perceive our body, mind and soul as a single unit.

Breath is associated with prana. We take in prana as we breathe in. In yoga philosophy, prana is the ultimate life force, "All of the energy present in the human body … The lack of prana leads to death" (A.G. Mohan). Prana is crucial for every living function and the right breathing is the means by which prana can be controlled and through which it can be worked.

THE BREATHING TECHNIQUE

Before concentrating on breathing techniques in power yoga, you should familiarise yourself with deep breathing.

- Observe how your abdomen rises and falls as you breathe deeply in and out.
- Close your mouth and breathe in and out through your nose.

It takes some effort to breathe like this, because a lot of energy is required to breathe in. It does, however, enable you to engage with your emotions!

Another breathing technique supports the detoxification of the body. Once you master this, you can breathe in deeply without exerting yourself. This type of breathing is preparation for ocean breathing:

- As you breathe out, expel as much air as possible from your lungs. Observe the movement of the diaphragm as you pull in your stomach and gentle pressure is placed on the lower part of the rib cage and the organs of the lower abdomen. The air now flows out of the lungs. Then relax your muscles. The lungs will then fill with air almost by themselves.

This breathing technique strengthens the diaphragm. Once you have practised this for a while, you are ready to move on to ocean breathing.

We have coined the term "ocean breathing" ourselves. In Ashtanga yoga, it is known as "Ujjayi". The noise produced by breathing in this way is redolent of waves breaking on the beach and flowing back to the ocean.

In power yoga, breathing is done exclusively through the nose. The mouth remains closed throughout the entire exercise phase, so that no energy is lost. The back of the throat is closed off slightly or the throat is narrowed. This causes the air to flow audibly over the vocal cords. By narrowing the throat, the experience of breathing becomes intense. Irregularities in breathing can be perceived through acoustic feedback (the sound produced) and corrected straight away.

Practise ocean breathing until you find your natural rhythm. Be patient with yourself – the effort is worthwhile!

BANDHAS AND REFINING BREATHING

The association of breathing techniques from power yoga with the use of bandhas requires a little more time.

Bandhas are blocks that are produced by tensing muscles. They are used to direct breathing and the flow of energy in the body. The bandhas increase the effectiveness of breathing in power yoga.
In power yoga, they are very important as they generate heat in the body and thereby support cleansing processes. Breathing exercises enable toxins in the body to be removed more easily; the bandhas enhance this process by directing the breath to places of toxins or tensions.

Power yoga actively uses two bandhas, the "Uddyana bandha" and the "Mula bandha".

Uddyana Bandha

When we breathe out, our navel is first drawn in towards the spine. Immediately before the next breath in, the navel is pulled further inwards and upwards, with both the diaphragm and the lower abdomen being raised. The muscles of the abdomen and the diaphragm touch and mutually strengthen each other.
If you release the uddyana bandha again, the upper abdomen and diaphragm relax. The muscle tension in the lower abdomen, however, is maintained. This automatically produces the mula bandha.

Mula Bandha

If the muscles below the navel are tensed together through the uddiyana bandha while the abdominal muscles above the navel remain relaxed, you activate the mula bandha by drawing the perineum upwards. The mula bandha works in the area of the pelvic floor.

Practise the bandhas correctly right from the start! It takes time to perfect the technique. But do not forget: the journey is the reward!

PRINCIPLES OF POWER YOGA

For power yoga to work effectively and for you to benefit quickly from what it offers, you should bear in mind the following principles when practising the exercises:

- Relax correctly: before and after practising, focus your awareness on your breathing and your thoughts should "flow" unhindered.
- Exercise correctly: there is a helpful exercise for every condition. It is best to exercise at the same time of day, ideally three times a week or, if you are able to and wish to, every day.
- Breathe correctly: with most exercises or asanas, breathing is performed deep into the abdomen. By concentrating on the correct breathing, the mind is cleared of disruptive thoughts and you can focus better on your exercises.
- Eat correctly: ideally, your diet should contain wholefoods or be vegetarian. The removal of meat and other animal proteins from your diet helps to maintain mobility.
- Think correctly and meditate: positive thinking is generally very important for a healthy body and mind. Meditation helps us to switch off, allowing us to recoup our strength for the challenges of everyday life.

BEFORE YOU BEGIN

Before starting power yoga training, you should talk to your doctor, especially

- if you are pregnant
- if you have just had surgery
- if you have had a serious illness
- if you have back injuries
- if you have high blood pressure
- if you feel weak
- if you have a chronic disease.

- Always practise power yoga barefoot so that your toes have a good grip and your feet can feel the ground (the use of a thin yoga mat can be helpful).
- Ensure that your weight is distributed evenly on your feet and that your spine is straight!
- The exercise room should be at a pleasant temperature and be well ventilated.
- Start the exercises slowly! Do not attempt too much at once; instead, progress with the programme step by step until you have mastered the individual series of exercises and are able to co-ordinate them with your breathing.
- Trust your feelings and stay "in touch" with your body. By doing this, you will find the intensity of exercise that is right for you.
- Be patient and do not over-exert yourself! This will enable you to carry out the exercises in a more insightful, gentle manner that is in harmony with your body's needs.
- Do not compare yourself with others! Everyone goes at their own pace. Adapt the exercises to your own rhythm.
- Only stretch your muscles as far as you feel comfortable!
- Mistakes that creep in when you start the exercises are hard to get rid of later on. So it is worth learning the exercises step by step. Practice each position until you master it and only work through the full programme once you have mastered the final exercise.

- Start off slowly. You can increase the pace once you have achieved the individual exercise sequences and the details of the movements. Discover your personal exercise rhythm and play with the speeds of the exercises. The more slowly you perform the exercises, the more difficult the training will be, since you need a lot of strength to breathe more slowly. If you wish to improve your performance, carry out the exercises quickly – simply adapt your speed to how you are feeling each day!

DEVELOPING WARMTH FROM WITHIN

Any successful and balanced physical training starts with a warm-up. The deep heat produced by this extends into the cells of the body, increasing their capacity to take up oxygen and firing up the metabolism. If the body is not warmed up, energy cannot flow freely through the joints, muscle fibres and organs. Only by ensuring a free flow of energy can blockades and tension be eliminated from the body. A gentle warm-up allows energy to flow through the muscles, slowly to begin with. The muscles are not put under great strain and the risk of injury is therefore minimised: how often do you hear of sporting injuries caused by too much stress being placed on "cold" muscles?

Sun Salutation I

Starting position or Mountain pose
(at least 5–10 repetitions)

The Mountain pose is the starting and end position for every exercise sequence in the Sun Salutation. The body assumes a deliberately upright posture. This enhances the feeling of stability.

- The feet are placed next to each other.
- The weight of the body is placed on the balls of the feet and centrally on the heels.
- The hands lie loosely on the thighs with the fingers lightly tensed.
- The shoulders are relaxed, the shoulder-blades drawn slightly together. This widens the rib cage and increases the volume of the lungs.
- The two bandhas (navel region and pelvic floor) are tensed.
- The pelvis is "tilted" slightly forwards and the chin inclined slightly downwards.
- The neck and back form a straight line.
- Focus on ocean breathing.
- Take ten deep breaths.

Focus on all of the components of the exercise. Make yourself familiar with the co-ordination of your breathing and posture. To begin with, only continue with the exercise sequence once you are consciously able to co-ordinate your breathing, bandhas and posture.

1st asana

- Breathe in.
- Stretch your arms out to the side and move them upwards until the palms of your hands touch.
- Tilt your head back slightly (not too far back!) with your gaze directed upwards.
- Tense the muscles of the thighs and raise your kneecaps slightly.
- Place your feet and toes flat and relaxed on the floor.
- Hold your back straight and feel the stretch!

2nd asana

- Breathe out.
- With your legs stretched out, extend your arms downwards until your fingertips touch the floor or, if possible, place your palms on the floor.
- Your head points towards your knee or touches it, with your gaze following the direction of your head.

TIP: Caution! If you have knee or back problems, bend your knees slightly!

3rd asana

- Breathe in.
- Lift your head slightly, keeping your spine stretched.
- Keep your knees straight if possible (or slightly bent).

4th asana, "Push-Up"

- Breathe out.
- Move to the push-up position by first setting your right foot, then your left foot, backwards (individuals with experience can jump to the push-up position with both feet simultaneously). Keep your upper body taut!
- Tense your buttocks. Do not allow your pelvis to sink! The elbows lie close to the body.
- Allow the upper body, pelvis and legs to "float" over the floor (if necessary, support yourself with your knees on the floor).
- Finally, direct your gaze forwards.

TIPS: Jump back to the push-up position only if you are experienced and do not have any back problems. If you have shoulder pain, take care not to allow the body to hang between the shoulder-blades when you move to the push-up position. If you do not have the strength to support your body, you can use your knees for support.

5th asana, "Upward-Facing Dog"

- Breathe in.
- Raise your upper body and "open your heart" (feel the expansion in your rib cage and allow energy to flow through the heart and the entire chest region).
- Roll your feet onto the instep, with the soles of your feet pointing upwards.
- Point the tips of your feet.
- Lie your palms flat on the floor.
- Tilt your head back slightly (not too far!).
- Your weight should be resting on your hands and the backs of your feet.

6th asana, "Downward-Facing Dog"

- Breathe out.
- Swing your hips upwards.
- Roll the feet back from the instep onto the toes, placing the feet parallel and at about a hip-width from each other.
- Place your palms flat on the floor with the fingers slightly spread.
- Allow the head to hang relaxed with your eyes looking towards your knees.
- The heels should rest, if possible, on the floor.
- Breathe in and out 5 times. Pay attention to the bandhas and your breathing.

TIP: Do not rotate your feet inwards, but instead keep them as straight as possible in order to achieve the best possible extension of the leg muscles!

7th asana

- Breathe in.
- First place the right, then the left foot between the hands (individuals who are experienced are able to jump with both feet forwards at the same time).
- The big toes should touch.
- Lift your head and stretch your back.
- The knees are straight or slightly bent.

8th asana

- Breathe out.
- Lower your upper body.
- Move your head towards your knees, drawing it towards your knees if possible.

9th asana

- Breathe in.
- Take your hands off the floor and straighten up your body.
- As you do so, move your arms upwards at the sides until your palms touch over your head.
- Lift your head.
- Tense your thighs.
- Stretch upwards.
- Strength shoots into the arms all the way to the fingertips.

Final position (Mountain pose)

- Breathe out.
- Lower your arms.
- Assume the Mountain pose and stand up straight.

Repeat the entire sequence 3 to 5 times, from the Mountain pose as the starting position to the Mountain pose as the final position.

BOOSTING ENERGY AND FINDING EQUILIBRIUM

Actual power yoga begins with exercises that are carried out while standing. They are especially efficient and boost the production of heat. Performing the Sun Salutation II as a warm-up is the best preparation for them. The aim of standing power yoga exercises is to achieve a high level of energy and vitality. They offer a way of achieving harmony with oneself in a dynamic way by accentuating the interaction of rhythm, symmetry and equilibrium.

Sun Salutation II

Mountain pose

- Stand up straight.
- Breathe in and out. Co-ordinate the bandhas and your breathing.

1st asana

- Breathe in.
- Bend your knees slightly.
- Move your arms outwards and upwards.
- Direct your gaze upwards.
- Place the palms of your hands together.

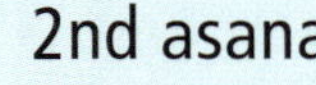

2nd asana

- Breathe out.
- Lower your arms and bend your upper body downwards.
- Keep your knees straight if possible.
- Move your arms backwards and place your hands on your heels.
- Draw your head towards your knees.
- Your gaze follows the movement of your head.

3rd asana

(This exercise is the same as the 3rd asana in Sun Salutation I.)

- Breathe in.
- Lift your upper body and head.
- Stretch your back.
- If possible, place your hands next to your feet on the floor.

4th asana, "Push-Up"

(This exercise is the same as the 4th asana in Sun Salutation I.)

- Breathe out.
- Move or jump to the push-up position.
- Keep your back straight.
- Direct your gaze forwards.

5th asana, "Upward-Facing Dog"

(This exercise is the same as the 5th asana in Sun Salutation I.)

- Breathe in.
- Push the body forwards and stretch out the tips of your toes.
- Raise the upper body and "open your heart".
- Your weight should be resting on your hands and the backs of your feet.
- Tilt your head back.

6th asana, "Downward-Facing Dog"

(This exercise is the same as the 6th asana in Sun Salutation I.)

- Breathe out.
- Swing upwards and roll your feet back onto your toes.
- Allow the head to hang relaxed.
- Direct your gaze towards your knees.
- The heels should rest, if possible, on the floor.

7th asana, "Warrior Pose I, Right"

- Breathe in.
- Place the right foot as far in front of you as you can.
- Turn the left foot inwards with the heel.
- Bend the right knee so that the upper and lower leg form a right angle.
- As you do so, straighten your upper body, move your arms upwards stretched out until your palms touch over your head.
- Push your hips forwards.
- Direct your gaze upwards.
- Hold this position for five breaths.

8th asana, "Push-Up"

- Breathe out.
- Lower your arms and place your palms on the floor.
- Move your right foot behind you.
- Lower the body into the push-up position.

9th asana, "Upward-Facing Dog"

- Breathe in.
- Push the body forwards, rolling your feet over your toes onto the instep.
- Widen your rib cage: "open your heart".
- Extend your arms, pull your shoulders back.
- Tilt your head back slightly.
- Your gaze follows the direction of your head.

10th asana, "Downward-Facing Dog"

- Breathe out.
- Stand on your tiptoes.
- Swing your hips upwards.
- Position your feet parallel at hip-width apart.
- Allow the head to hang relaxed with your eyes looking towards your knees.
- The heels should rest, if possible, on the floor.

11th asana, "Warrior Pose I, left"

- Breathe in.
- Place the left foot as far in front of you as you can.
- Turn the right foot inwards with the heel at an angle.
- Bend the left knee.
- Straighten your upper body.
- Move your arms upwards stretched out until your palms touch over your head.
- Direct your gaze upwards.
- Hold this position for five breaths.

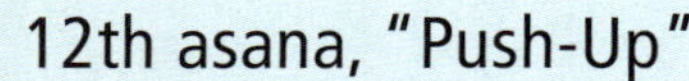

12th asana, "Push-Up"

- Breathe out.
- Lower your arms and place your palms on the floor.
- Move your right foot behind you.
- Lower the body into the push-up position.

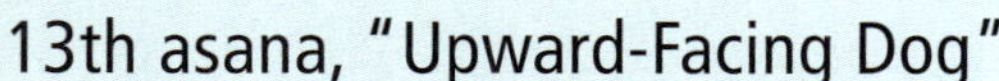

13th asana, "Upward-Facing Dog"

- Breathe in.
- Push the body forwards, rolling your feet over your toes onto the instep.
- Widen your rib cage, "open your heart".
- Extend your arms, pull your shoulders back.
- Tilt your head back slightly.
- Your gaze follows the direction of your head.

14th asana, "Downward-Facing Dog"

- Breathe out.
- Stand on your tip toes.
- Swing your hips upwards.
- Position your feet parallel at hip-width apart.
- Allow the head to hang relaxed with your eyes looking towards your knees.
- The heels should rest, if possible, on the floor.
- Breathe in and out 5 times.

15th asana

- Breathe in.
- Place your feet forwards or jump forwards with both feet.
- Stretch your legs out.
- Your palms, if possible, should touch the floor or lie on your ankles.
- Lift your head, stretch your back.

16th asana

(This exercise is the same as the 2nd asana in Sun Salutation I).

- Breathe out.
- Bend the upper body downwards.
- Draw your head towards your knees.

17th asana

(This exercise is the same as the 1st asana in Sun Salutation I.)

- Breathe in.
- Bend your knees.
- Straighten up your body.
- Move your arms upwards until your palms touch.
- Direct your gaze upwards.

Mountain pose

- Breathe out.
- Move your arms downwards.
- Assume the Mountain pose and stand up straight.

Repeat the entire sequence 3 to 5 times.

TIP: If you are not very strong, the Sun Salutation is the ideal way of building up strength. You should move on to the subsequent power yoga exercises once you have succeeded with Sun Salutation I and II, i. e. have mastered the sequence of positions and transitions and are familiar with ocean breathing.

One-Legged Squat

- Breathe out.
- Bend forwards, stretching your arms down towards your feet.
- Grasp your big toes with your index fingers and thumbs.
- Draw your upper body towards your thighs.
- Tense the thigh extensors (muscles on the front of the thigh).
- The knees are not pressed down.
- Breathe in and out 5 times.

- Breathe in.
- Stretch your back, lift your head and widen your rib cage slightly.
- Breathe out.
- Draw your upper body back towards your thighs.
- The bandhas are tensed.
- Remain in this position for five breaths.

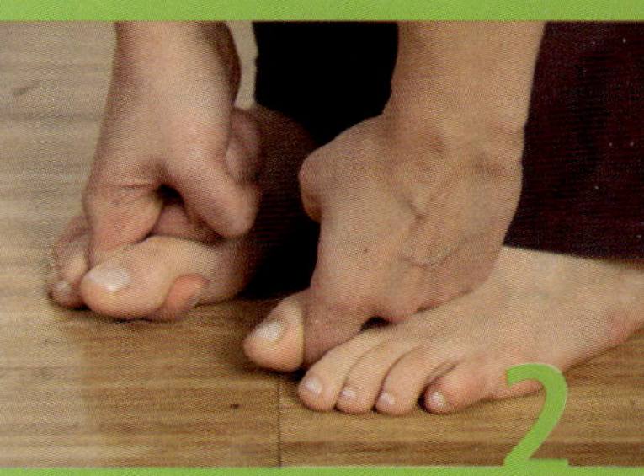

- Breathe in.
- Straighten up, move your arms out sideways and upwards.
- Breathe out.
- Stand up straight.

TIP FOR BEGINNERS: If you are not very agile yet, carry out this exercise with your knees bent. Hold the position for just three breaths, instead of the recommended five.
If you have back or knee problems, bend your knees slightly before lowering your upper body! By tensing the bandhas as you bend forwards, you can protect your back from over-extension. Always bend from the hip forwards, holding your back straight and ensuring that your shoulders are relaxed!

Elongated Triangle, Left and Right Side

- Breathe in.
- Place your feet about 1 metre apart.
- Stretch your arms out to the side horizontally.
- Rotate your right foot 90° outwards and rotate your left foot slightly inwards.

- Breathe out.
- Bend your upper body downwards over your right side until your thumb and index finger grip your big toe.
- Tense your right thigh and the bandhas.

- Stretch your left arm straight upwards.
- Align your head upwards, with your gaze resting on your outstretched hand.
- Hold this position for five breaths.

- Breathe in.
- Straighten up, with your arms stretched out to the side.
- Carry out the "Elongated Triangle" exercise on the other side.
- Breathe out.
- Tense the bandhas.

TIP FOR BEGINNERS: If you are not very mobile yet, you can simply grab your ankle with your hand instead. Do not try forcing yourself to grip your toes!

Warrior Pose II, Right Side

- Breathe in.
- Rotate the hip and the right foot to the right.
- Your gaze should also move to the right.
- Keep your torso facing forwards.
- Move your arms upwards. Place your hands together. Point your fingertips upwards.

- Breathe out.
- Bend your knee and lower yourself far to the right in this position.
- Keep your gaze on your outstretched right arm.

- Hold this position for five breaths.

- Breathe in.
- Come back up to the middle.

- Breathe out.

Warrior Pose II, Left Side

- Breathe in.
- Turn your feet now to the other side.
  Direct your gaze to the left.
  Keep your torso facing forwards.
- Breathe out.
- Bend your knee and lower yourself far to the left in this position.
- Keep your gaze on your outstretched left arm.
- Hold this position for five breaths.
- Breathe in.
- Come back to the middle as before.
- Breathe out.

Elongated Side Angle, Right and Left Side

- Breathe in.
- Place the feet parallel with each other 1 metre apart.
- Stretch your arms out to the side.
- Turn your right foot outwards and your left foot inwards.

- Breathe out.
- Bend your right knee and extend the upper body downwards to the right-hand side.
- Place your right hand on the outside of your foot.
- Stretch your left arm far over your head, fully extending your left leg.
- Focus your gaze up towards your hand.
- Do not hold your breath and tense the bandhas!

- Hold this position for five breaths.

- Breathe in.
- Straighten up.
- Turn to the left.
- Place your feet parallel to each other.

- Carry out the "Elongated Side Angle" exercise on the other side.

TIP FOR BEGINNERS: Place your right hand on the inside of your right foot instead of the outside. If you find it difficult to begin with, you can also place your arm bent on your right knee and support yourself that way.

Intense Spread Leg Stretch

- Breathe in.
- Place your feet as far apart as possible.
- Place your hands on your waist.
- Tilt your head back (not too far back).
- Draw your shoulder-blades together.
- Tense your thighs: your bandhas have become active.

- Breathe out.
- Bend forwards until your hands touch the floor.
- Keep your back straight.
- Pull your upper body downwards between your legs so that your head is between your hands.
- The thigh muscles and bandhas remain active.

- Hold this position for five breaths.

- Breathe in.
- Lift your head and chest.

- Breathe out.
- Place your hands on your waist.

- Breathe in.
- Straighten up and bend backwards.
- Draw your shoulder-blades together again, tilt your head back.
- The thighs and the bandhas remain tensed.

- Breathe out.
- Come forwards.
- Keep your hands on your waist.
- Draw your upper body as far down as you can between your legs.

- Remain in this position for five breaths.

- Breathe in.
- Come back up again and stretch your arms out to the side as you do.

- Breathe out.
- Tense your thighs.

- Breathe in.
- Draw the shoulder-blades together and cross your arms behind your back.

- Breathe out.
- Come forwards and, if you can, rotate your hands outwards.
- Keep your back straight.
- Do not lift your neck; your head should hang loosely between your shoulders.
- The bandhas are active.

- Remain in this position for five breaths.

- Breathe in.
- Come upwards, lifting your head and chest.

- Breathe out.
- Place your hands back on your waist.

- Breathe in.
- Look up, press your shoulder-blades together, extend your rib cage by bending backwards slightly.
- The thighs and the bandhas are tensed.

- Breathe out.
- Bend forwards, grip your big toes with your thumbs and forefingers.
- Draw your upper body downwards, if possible to between your legs.
- The elbows are angled so that the shoulders remain relaxed.

- Remain in this position for five breaths.

- Breathe in.
- Straighten up, place your hands back on your waist.

- Breathe out.
- Place your feet parallel to each other.
- Relax your arms.
- Stand up straight.

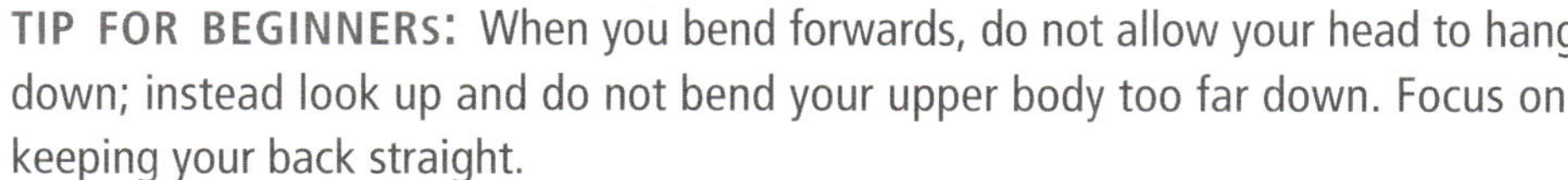

TIP FOR BEGINNERS: When you bend forwards, do not allow your head to hang down; instead look up and do not bend your upper body too far down. Focus on keeping your back straight.
If you cannot touch the floor with your hands, place them on your thigh.

Rib Cage Expansion

- Breathe in.
- Place your feet around 1 metre apart.
- Place your hands on your back so that your palms are vertically next to each other (you can also cross your forearms behind your back and hold them with your hands).
- Extend backwards and widen your rib cage.
- Breathe out.
- Bend forwards.
- If possible, make your chin touch your knee.
- Your gaze is directed at your feet.
- Keep your back straight.
- The bandhas are active.
- Remain in this position for five breaths.

Variation with side extension

- Breathe in.
- Straighten up and bend backwards.
- Breathe out.
- Turn your feet, pelvis and torso to the right.
- Bend forwards, towards your knee.
- Hold this position for five breaths.
- Breathe in.
- Come back up, place your feet parallel to each other.
- Breathe out.
- Perform the exercise on the left-hand side.
- Stand up straight.

Tree, Right and Left Side

- Breathe in.
- Bend your right leg, placing your foot on the inside of the left thigh.
- The thigh and the bandhas are tensed.
- Move your hands upwards and bring your palms together over your head.

- Breathe out.
- Look straight ahead.
- Focus on maintaining your balance.
- Hold this position for three breaths.
- Breathe out.
- Come out of the position.
- Stand up straight.

- Repeat the exercise with the left leg.
- Hold this position for three breaths.
- Breathe out.
- Come out of the position.
- Stand up straight.

REACHING THE FORCE CENTRE

The exercises in power yoga that are carried out on the floor result in self-centring by synchronising movement and breathing and increasing concentration. The exercises on the floor cause energy to flow more and more freely through the body: we become alert and aware. By becoming calmer, we can establish a harmonious relationship with ourselves and the world around us.

Four-Legged Stance or "Cat"

- Breathe in.
- Get on all fours.
- Place your lower legs on the ground so that a right angle is formed between them and your thighs.
- Tilt your head back slightly, allowing your spine to sink down to produce a small hollow.
- Pull your buttocks upwards slightly.
- Keep your shoulders straight.
- Breathe out.
- Now slowly stretch your spine and form an arch.
- Stretch into the arch until your back becomes round.
- Tense the bandhas.
- Allow the head to hang relaxed.
- Rest on your lower legs, stretch your hands far out in front of you over your head.
- Remain in this position for five breaths.
- Breathe in.
- Come back up.
- Breathe out.
- Get on all fours.
- Repeat the exercise 3 times.
- Breathe in.
- Draw in one leg after the other and move them forwards until both are lying on the floor.
- Breathe out.
- Sit straight.

Forwards Bending

- Breathe in.
- Stretch your arms upwards.
- Place the palms of your hands together.

- Breathe out.
- Bend your upper body forwards and grip your big toes with your thumbs and index fingers (or place your hands on your ankles).

- Breathe in.
- Your back remains stretched; your head is tilted back slightly.
- Direct your gaze upwards.
- The bandhas and leg muscles are tensed.
- Remember ocean breathing!

- Breathe out.
- Now bend your elbows, pulling yourself downwards with your upper arms.
- Place your chin on your knees, keeping your back straight.
- Tense the bandhas and thigh muscles.
- Focus your gaze on your toes.

- Remain in this position for five breaths.

Backwards Bending

- Breathe in.
- Place your palms on the floor behind you, with your fingers relaxed.
- Breathe out.

- Raise yourself up until your body forms a straight line.
- Draw your shoulder blades together slightly and expand your rib cage.
- The thighs are tensed.
- Hold this position for five breaths.

- Breathe in.
- Maintain this tension.
- Breathe out.
- Come out of the position and return to sitting.

Half Lotus, Right and Left Side

- Breathe in.
- Bend your right leg.
- Breathe out.
- Place your right foot on your left thigh with the inside of your foot pointing upwards.
- Breathe in.
- Move your arms upwards, lift your head, stretch your back.
- Breathe out.
- Bend far forwards, keeping your back straight.
- Draw your upper body downwards.
- Move your head towards your knees.
- Tense your extended thigh.
- Focus your gaze on your feet.
- Remain in this position for five breaths.
- Breathe in.
- Move your arms upwards, lift your head, stretch your back.
- Breathe out.
- Stretch out your bent leg.
- Sit.
- Carry out the "Half Lotus" exercise on the other side.

Half Lotus Sideways, Right and Left Side

- Breathe in.
- Stretch out your left leg.
- Place your right foot on the inside of your left thigh.
- Grip your left foot with your left hand.

- Breathe out.
- Move your right arm in an arch over your head and extend it.
- Feel the extension.
- Breathe into the extended side.

- Remain in this position for five breaths.

- Breathe in
- Straighten up your upper body.
- Breathe out.
- Come out of the position.
- Return to the starting position.

- Carry out the "Half Lotus" exercise on the other side.

Bound Angle

- Breathe in.
- Place the soles of the feet against each other and turn the undersides upwards.
- Hold your feet with your hands.
- Stretch your spine, drawing your shoulders back slightly.
- Breathe out.

- Bend your upper body forwards from the hip so the tip of your nose points towards the floor.
- Remain in this position for five breaths.
- Breathe in.
- Come up.
- Breathe out.
- Come out of the position and sit.

RESTING

Continue to focus on the bandhas and the static muscle contractions.

Ensure you carry out ocean breathing calmly and at a regular rate. Do not allow your concentration to lapse, in order to maintain the heat.

Lying down

- Breathe in.
- Straighten up the spine.

- Breathe out.
- Come out of the seated position and slowly glide to the floor.
- Stretch your arms out to the side.
- Spread your legs slightly.
- Ensure that your body position is symmetrical.
- Direct your gaze upwards.

- Remain in this position for at least ten breaths or longer.

Supine Sideways Twist to the Right and Left

- Breathe in.
- Bend the left knee, guiding your foot towards your right knee.
- Keep your buttocks on the floor.
- Keep your arms in the same position.
- The head remains straight, with your gaze focused upwards.

- Breathe out.
- Extend the knee to the right towards the floor.
- The foot remains on the right knee.
- The bandhas and right thigh are tensed.
- Turn your head to the left.

- Hold this position for five breaths.

- Breathe in.
- Swing the leg back up again.

- Breathe out.
- Come back to the middle and stretch out both legs.

- Carry out the "Supine Sideways Twist" exercise on the other side.

TIP: If you cannot keep your knee down to begin with, press your knee gently downwards with your hand. Note that your head should remain on the floor!

Shoulder Bridge

- Breathe in.
- Bend your legs.

- Breathe out.
- Place your feet firmly on the floor.

- Breathe in.
- Stretch your arms out backwards in an arc and lay them on the floor.
- Push your pelvis upwards so that your weight is distributed evenly over your shoulders and feet.
- The bandhas and thigh muscles are active.

- Breathe out.
- Bring the arms back downwards in an arc next to the body.
- Keep the pelvis up as long as you can.

- Hold this position for three breaths.

- Breathe in.

- Breathe out.
- Lower your pelvis until your buttocks are once again on the floor.

Shoulder Stand

- Breathe in.

- Draw up your knees.

- Breathe out.
- Stretch the legs straight out and upwards.

- Breathe in.
- Lift your buttocks.
- Support your body with your hands.
- Lift your legs over your head with the tips of the toes drawn downwards.

- Remain in this position for five breaths.

- Breathe in.
- Bend your legs.

- Breathe out.
- Keep your back straight and continue to support yourself.
- Stretch your legs vertically upwards.
- The tips of your toes point upwards.
- The bandhas and thighs are active.

- Remain in this position for five breaths.

TIP: Caution! The Shoulder Stand should not be performed if you are pregnant, are menstruating, have high blood pressure or have neck problems.

- Breathe in.
- Bend your knees slightly.

- Breathe out.
- Stretch your legs out and bring them behind your head until the tips of your toes touch the floor or at least point towards the floor.

- Experienced individuals can lower their knees next to their ears.
- Place your arms on the floor and stretch them out.

- Remain in this position for five breaths.

- Breathe in.
- Slowly unroll the spine, keeping your legs extended.
- The bandhas and thigh muscles are active.

- Breathe out.
- Lay your legs stretched out on the floor.

- Breathe in.
- Bend your legs.

- Breathe out.
- Come up to the sitting position; grasp your knees with your hands.

After this cool-down, do not stop your training, but instead move to the closing positions.

REFINEMENT AND EXPERIENCING INTEGRATION

The following exercises promote inner harmony, liberate the mind and create new insights into the world of emotions. The body cools down slowly, you are calm and you achieve a state of complete relaxation. Energy flows through every organ and every cell in the body. You feel light, relaxed and at the same time euphoric.

The closing positions allow us to gather the energy we have built up during training. This makes the body calm. It is still important at this stage to maintain our concentration, so that we do not lose any of our inner warmth.

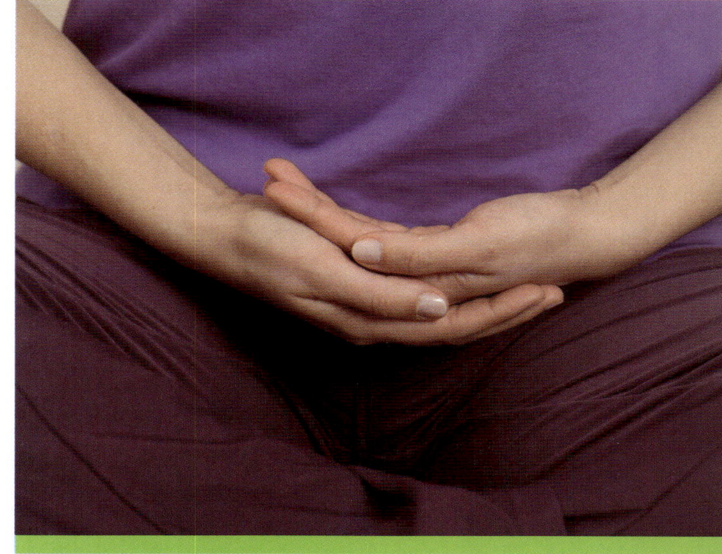

2

Lotus with Crossed Hands

- Sit.
- Breathe in.
- Draw up your right or left foot, placing the inside of the foot upwards on the thigh of the other leg.

- Breathe out.
- The heel rests in the groin and presses gently against the lower abdomen.

- Breathe in.
- Draw up the second foot, lay it over the other leg, with the inside of the foot facing upwards on the thigh.

- Breathe out.
- The heel presses gently into the lower abdomen.

- Breathe in.
- Move your hands behind you and cross them.

- Breathe out.
- If possible, rotate the palms of your crossed arms outwards.
- Move your upper body forwards.
- Your forehead should also point towards the floor.

- Remain in this position for five breaths.

- Breathe in.
- Straighten your upper body.

- Breathe out.
- Release your hands and place them on your knees.

Resting Lotus

- Breathe in.
- Place your hands with your palms facing upwards on your knees, with your thumb and forefinger forming a circle or, if you prefer, simply leave your palms open.
- Stretch your spine.
- Consciously expand your rib cage.

- Breathe out.
- Your shoulders are relaxed.
- Your chin is pulled slightly downwards.
- Your eyes are only half-open.
- Find a point in front of you on the floor and focus on it.
- The bandhas are tensed.

- Remain in this position for ten breaths or longer.

Scale Pan Pose

- Breathe in.
- Join your hands loosely.
- Then place your palms next to your body on the floor.

- Breathe out.
- Sit up and draw your knee slightly towards your body.
- Look forwards.
- The bandhas are active.

- Then powerfully and quickly expel the air from your lungs ten times (fire breathing)!

- Breathe in.

- Breathe out.
- Come out of the position.
- Slowly extend your legs and move to the lying position.

TIP: Fire breathing (similar to hyperventilation) is a technique that can release unwanted emotions. You may feel dizzy.
Approach the exercise carefully, ideally in the presence of a teacher who will help you to integrate the feelings that come to the surface.

Resting Pose

The Resting Pose is the most important position in all power yoga training, as without it you will not be able to absorb the unleashed energy to the full. Make sure you set aside enough time to assume this pose! It is the pose that is hardest to master.

- The arms lie along the body, the legs lie parallel next to each other or are slightly spread. Maintain symmetry.
- Your chin is pulled slightly downwards.
- Close your eyes.
- Relax your body, transferring your weight to the floor.
- Lie yourself down so that nothing disturbs you.
- All your tension dissolves.
- Your breathing flows regularly and calmly.

- Do not succumb to the temptation to fall asleep. Stay awake!

- Remain in the rest position for 5–10 minutes.

Deep within us there is something untouchable, something true, that never changes. In yoga, this is known as "the third eye". Often, we are unaware that this force is guiding us. It is as though we are swimming in a river, are unable to see the banks and therefore do not perceive the flow of the current. If we connect with this force, however, if we notice how it guides us, we can allow ourselves to be carried by it. Performing power yoga means doing precisely this.

"When I am wide awake, in the middle of the day, my most fantastic dreams come true."

LORENZ HART

The small rush

Lying down, you can feel overcome by the energies released – you may lose the sensation of the ground beneath you and experience a feeling of floating. Energy is circulating throughout your body; your spine feels like an electric rod (Kundalini, the coiled force, is developing: from your bottom at the lowest chakra at the base of the spine, it pervades all of the body's energy centres up into the skull area). You may see flashing lights in front of your closed eyelids. And yet your mind is clear and calm. You are completely relaxed and enjoying a state of complete presence of mind!

When you stand up and open your eyes, you will see the world with different eyes. You will feel light and unburdened. Your eyes will shine. You have worked intensively on yourself and your body. The people around you will literally feel your energy and feel magnetically drawn to you. Take this freshness and alertness with you in your life and share it with others!

MEDITATION TECHNIQUES AND BREATHING EXERCISES

> "Yoga therapy is only preparation for the true experience of yoga, which allows us to find new opportunities for personal development."
>
> GARY KRAFTSOW, "YOGA FOR WELLNESS"

Breathing exercises

Specific breathing exercises or pranayama help us to step up the cleansing processes within our body and mind. Do not practise them before power yoga training, but rather afterwards or separately.

The exercises are best carried out while sitting. If you have problems sitting for long periods on the floor, sit on a chair or stand up. It is important to keep your spine straight!

Now try to develop a hard and soft breathing pattern. Your mind becomes calm and your emotions stabilise.
The old yoga masters believed that they could direct the ebb and flow of emotions through the controlled breath that they allowed to flow through their noses. Breathing in through the right nostril and breathing out through the left one activates and stimulates us; performing the exercise the other way round calms us.

Here are a few examples of how long you should breathe in and out for – the numbers represent seconds. Start as follows:

8 (breathe in) – 0 (hold your breath) – 8 (breathe out) – 0 (hold your breath);
8–0–16–0;
7–3–7–3;
etc.

Try to find a breathing rhythm that suits you. To discover one, you should first practise for a while or consult an experienced yoga teacher. The teacher can give you the confidence to know that you are not over-exerting yourself or pushing your limits without external support.
The exercise can also release suppressed emotions and memories – so be prepared for this!

Fire breathing for strong nerves

Following on from the last exercise, you can practise fire breathing: this harmonises the body, mind and soul. The blood circulates in the lower back areas, strengthening the spine and the organs of the lower body. You become focused, attentive and alert and at the same time you are calm and relaxed inside.

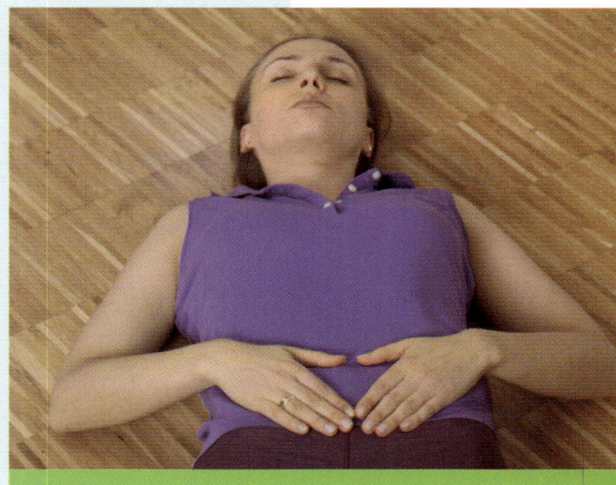

- Breathe in and clasp your hands together.
- Focus on activating the bandhas and breathe in and out in a staccato fashion 10 times.
- Expel the air powerfully and quickly from your lungs.
- Relax and allow your breath to flow calmly.
- You should then lie down for a while and allow the energy released to circulate around your body.

Pranayama

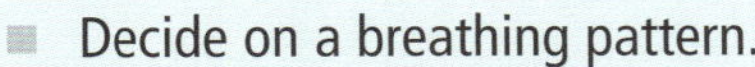

- Decide on a breathing pattern.
- If you are unsure of which one to choose, try 5–1–7–1. This is a simple, straightforward breathing rhythm.
- Do not hold your breath too long after breathing in!
- Sit either cross-legged, in the Half Lotus pose or in the Lotus position.

- Place your right thumb on your right nostril.
- Keep your back straight.
- Rest your free hand relaxed on your knee.
- Your chin is pulled slightly downwards.
- Tense the bandhas.

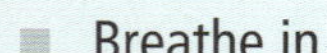

- Breathe in.
- The right nostril is closed by your thumb.
- Breathe slowly through the left nostril, and your breath circulates around the spine downwards to its base.
- Count to five (5).
- Hold your breath briefly (1).

- Breathe out.
- Now place your left thumb on your left nostril.
- Count to seven (7).
- Your breath circulates upwards around the spine.
- The bandhas are active.
- Accustom yourself to this position for a moment (1).

- Practise this for around 5–10 minutes.
- You should carry out this exercise in exactly the reverse order to achieve inner calm!

With these exercises, you have created the ideal foundations for meditation. Empty your mind. Your nerves will become calm as you do so.

Closing meditation

During meditation, you will gain distance from everything going through your mind and let go of emotional experiences.

- Simply sit still or choose a mantra – a short, formulaic sequence of words that you can repeat in your head and on which your mind can focus. Note the position of your hands!

- Open your hands (the energy circle is open, absorbing energy from outside).
- Allow your hands to rest on your knees.

- Bring your thumb and index finger together in a ring shape.

Open meditation

Open meditation is not concerned with any special meditation subject. It produces deep relaxation and releases you from worries and cares, clears your head and opens up the heart and mind to new stimulus. This type of meditation is suitable for all and promotes a "higher" perspective on things.

- Sit comfortably and ensure that you are able to breathe in and out freely.
- Your spine should be as straight or upright as possible.
- Pull your chin slightly downwards, so that your back and head form a straight line.
- Close your eyes.
- Focus on your inner calm, relaxing sounds or a mantra, so that your mind can attach itself to a "vehicle" rather than specific thoughts, and therefore relax better.
- Remain alert and attentive inside.
- Focus on breathing in and out regularly and deeply.
- Imagine that your breath, as you breathe in, is a cool draught of air flowing along your spine down to your coccyx.
- As you breathe out, your breath flows back upwards and exits through your nose. Relax very deeply.

TIP: Form a padded corner out of cushions and a soft blanket. From now on, this is the place where you can relax and rediscover yourself, indulge yourself or find solace. A protected space for your soul and an oasis of relaxation for your body and mind. Try to give your corner a defined place in your home and keep the cushion arrangement as a permanent "energy zone" fixture for yourself. It is where you will gain new energy and find inner calm.

Meditation of the senses

Meditation of the senses has a specific meditation object and stimulates a passion for life, well-being and creativity, regardless of whether you are meditating on the beauty of a blade of grass or the wideness of the sky. It vitalises our sensual side and is ideal for people who feel empty inside.

- Sit upright and relaxed.
- Close your eyes.
- Breathe in and out deeply.
- Accentuate your meditation with positive internal images and ideas that stimulate your senses.
- Paint a picture with colours, smells and sounds so that it is as sensual and lively as possible.
- Whether you're dreaming of beaches, the sea or a wonderful meal: luxuriate in this wonderful concept for as long as you like without heeding the critical voice of reason. Simply switch off unpleasant thoughts.
- It helps to also free yourself from disruptive thoughts with an affirmation, a positive statement. Say to yourself: "I enjoy my life."
- Consciously feel the positive effect on your body and mind.
- There is no longer any room for negative thoughts.
- You feel light and unburdened.
- Very soon, you will be much more relaxed and feel clear and refreshed.

TIP: An aroma oasis in the home: add wonderful-smelling scented essences to an aroma lamp (bergamot, lemon, mandarin, cinnamon or similar) or light joss sticks or incense. Scents and aromas distribute a pleasant atmosphere and work wonders when it comes to physical and spiritual well-being.

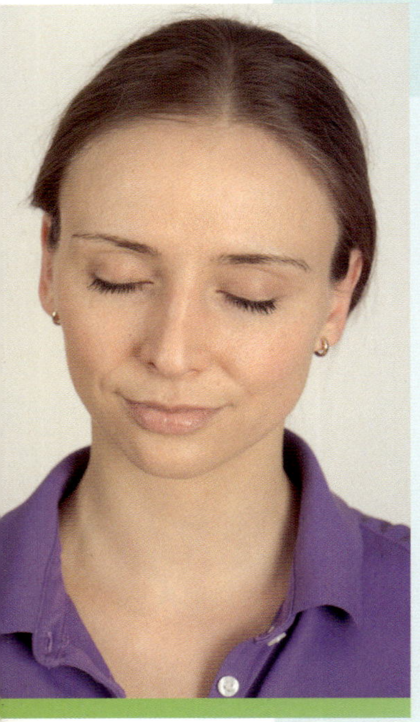

Yoga for the eyes and ears

This exercise helps to relax the eyes and face. It can be carried out as and when or following the power yoga programme, during the closing exercises. Following it, your eyes are refreshed and you see the world very differently.

- Close your eyes.
- Remember to breathe in and out calmly and deeply.
- Place the tips of your middle fingers slightly above your eyebrows in the centre of the forehead and circle them with light pressure over the sensitive pressure point a few times in succession.
- As you do so, allow the muscles of your chin to relax and do not hold your breath. If you have headaches or tension, this exercise can really work wonders, while the facial features relax.
- Then use both fingertips to stroke your temples and tauten your forehead. Repeat this several times.
- Allow your fingertips to rest for a moment on your temples and then press them at short intervals several times in succession.
- This activates energy processes and decongests the tissues.
- Open your eyes.
- Now glide towards your earlobes, massage them and then knead the whole of your ear, little by little.
- To finish, stroke the lymph pathways on the outsides of your neck using your fingertips, making powerful movements from top to bottom.
- Repeat this exercise several times also.

TIP: The tea ceremony: after relaxation or closing exercises in yoga, the body sometimes feels slightly cool, so it is the perfect time for a hot cup of tea. Calmly prepare a good (herb) tea that has a smooth taste. Then go to a beautiful place within your own four walls, sit down and make yourself comfortable. Now you're allowed to abandon yourself to relaxation. The wonderful scent of the tea stimulates your senses, which have suddenly become delicate and fragile. A gift like a new day that you can welcome with joy.

Enjoy this moment of calm, which can create a bridge between the world of yoga, deep relaxation and your everyday life. Now take the strength you have gained and your good mood into your life, as it will help you to retain your inner calm and serenity for a while longer!

We wish you every success as you carry out your power yoga programme, and we hope it brings you serenity and positive energy!

Authors

Barbara Klein, Ulrike Lowis, Claudia Pfeiffer, Robert S. Polster, Michael Sauer, Jutta Schuhn, Christa G. Traczinski, Sylvia Winnewisser

Picture credits

Mike Harter: P 17, 26, 31–34, 36–44, 46–48, 50–54, 56–63, 65, 70, 74–76, 78–80, 82, 83 bottom, 84;
Tilo Wiedensohler: P 35, 85, 87, 89, 94–122, 124–134, 136–143;
energyzone: P 5, 6, 86 (Patrick Baier), 135;
www.fotolia.com: P 7 (rebvt), 15 (EastWest Imaging), 21 (tsach), 81 (Alex Bramwell), 88 (chinatiger), 90 (Bernd S), 92 (dean sanderson), 93 (Olga Lyubkina);
mauritius images: P 19, 23, 45, 123, 144;
Shutterstock.com: P 25 (Artur Bogacki), 28 (Andrejs Pidjass), 64 (Kristian Sekulic) 66 (Kristian Sekulic), 68–69 (Sean Nel), 71 (Dimitrije Paunovic), 72 (alcaline), P 83 top (Sean Nel);
Thema Media: P 11;
Prof. Peter Thiele: P 29;
Eberhard Thiem: P 14